D0637497

BX
4827.B3
W69

KARL BARTH

KARL BARTH

AN ECUMENICAL APPROACH
TO HIS THEOLOGY

by

Dr. B. A. Willems, O.P.

Translated by

Matthew J. van Velzen

DEUS BOOKS
PAULIST PRESS
(Paulist Fathers)
Glen Rock, N.J.

BX 4827 B3 1965
Willems, Boniface A
Karl Barth: an ecumenical

A Deus Books Edition of the Paulist Press, 1965, by special arrangement with Lannoo Publishers, Tielt and The Hague.

NIHIL OBSTAT: Robert E. Hunt, S.T.D.
Censor Librorum

IMPRIMATUR: ✠ Thomas A. Boland, S.T.D.
Archbishop of Newark

June 2, 1965

The Nihil Obstat and Imprimatur are official declarations that a book or pamphlet is free of doctrinal or moral error. No implication is contained therein that those who have granted the Nihil Obstat and Imprimatur agree with the contents, opinions or statements expressed.

English Translation Copyright © 1965 by
The Missionary Society
of St. Paul the Apostle
in the State of New York

Library of Congress
Catalog Card Number: 65-24044 ✔

COVER DESIGN: Claude Ponsot

Published by the Paulist Press
Editorial Office: 304 W. 58th St., N.Y., N.Y. 10019
Business Office: Glen Rock, New Jersey 07452

Manufactured in the
United States of America

24

About the Author

Dr. B. A. Willems, O. P., was born December 4, 1926, at Rotterdam. He joined the Dominican Order in 1945 and was ordained a priest in 1952. After obtaining his doctorate at Münster under Hermann Volk, with a thesis on the necessity of the Church for salvation, he studied at Basel under Karl Barth, and then in Strasbourg. He taught Ecclesiology at the Dominican House of Studies at Zwolle. At present he teaches Dogma at the Albertinum College, Nijmegen.

Contents

9

CONTENTS

Introduction

"Talking *about* somebody leads with a fatal necessity to *passing over* him and closing his grave more firmly."

These words of Karl Barth in his Preface to the third edition of his *Römerbrief* (*Epistle to the Romans*) may be understood as a verdict on all those who would sketch a biography, and also, therefore, on the one who would sketch a biography of Karl Barth himself. Nevertheless, the minister of Safenwil, in the rual Canton of Aargau (Switzerland), has written his *Römerbrief* and attempted to present in it Paul's profoundest vision of Christian reality. In so doing, he has most emphatically not meant to write *about* Paul, but has tried to gain a deeper understanding of him.

To do this one needs a sympathetic approach, he must enter into the mind of his subject. Otherwise, he merely nails the person he is writing about, like some lifeless object, to the paradigm of his own philosophy of life. In such a case one may prove much, perhaps, and always have the highest right on his side, but the highest right is then also the highest injustice.

When Antoine de Saint-Exupéry made his lovable little prince say that one can only see really well with one's heart, he was merely expressing what Goethe had already written in a letter to Jacobi: one only knows what one loves. And at that time also this was not a new discovery.

Therefore, to write about Barth without doing him injustice requires a sympathetic approach. There are obvious traits in Barth that might well render such an approach difficult. As a Catholic writing about Barth, one might feel stung by his remarks on the occasion of the founding of the World Council of Churches at Amsterdam. It is definitely not pleasant to have to hear that our absence there saved the ecumenical movement a scandal as well as a temptation. Nor is it entirely pleasant to read in the Preface to the first volume of the *Kirchliche Dogmatik* (*Church Dogmatics*) the now famous statement: "I consider the *analogia entis* (analogy of being) as an invention of the antichrist, and I think that for this reason alone one cannot become a Catholic."

However, it is precisely for these and similar statements, which have been carefully polished up and pushed to their extremes by shortsighted and stubborn apologetics, that the rule counts that one has no right to nail the speaker to them. True, one has to take them seriously. There is no more frustrating way to break off communications than when one does not

take the other person seriously and relegates everything he says to the realm of "not meant so seriously".
On the other hand, one must not tear some statements
loose from the living background in which they were
spoken. Even when one does not agree with somebody—and perhaps precisely then in a high degree—
communication and a sympathetic approach are possible. Equal poles repel one another. Only when
each party brings his own original contribution into
the dialogue does it become a genuine human
encounter.

Barth is not inaccessible for such an approach. He
represents an idea. He does not do this as some
inanimate, unemotional, bookish scholar, but as a
human being with a remarkably rich, sensitive life.
His admiration for Mozart, which some Dutch
theologians judged so disapprovingly that they pro-
voked Barth to risk some venomous sentence about it
in his *Kirchliche Dogmatik,* is characteristic of him.
After discussions with Hans Urs von Balthasar, who
was working on his now-famous book on Barth, it
sometimes became necessary around midnight to play
some records in order to cool down their overheated
theological minds. Bart's admiration for Mozart is so
great that he once said that when he goes to Heaven
he will first ask for Mozart and only then for Augustine, Luther, Calvin and Schleiermacher. Apart from
his sentiments for Mozart, Barth also has a great
sense of humor. While it is not always the keen
French wit (*esprit*) that sparkles in his writings, it
is certainly not the crude fun (*Spass*) of Luther's
Tischreden (Table-Talk). As a Swiss, perhaps, Barth
has something of both, although the French understand him less easily than the Germans. In addition

to outspoken enemies Karl Barth also has many friends. His friendship with Eduard Thurneysen, who was until recently his fellow professor on the Basel theological faculty, has already lasted for over fifty years. Such a personality must possess qualities that make it possible to communicate with him on the human level.

This is exactly what will be attempted in the following pages. Obviously we could not discuss all the aspects of Barth's rich personality, nor all the facets—not even all the most important ones—of his doctrinal opinions. We can only hope that the resulting broad picture does not disfigure the great theologian Karl Barth too much. Wherever possible, we will let him speak for himself.

We acknowledge at the outset our indebtedness to a few works, which at the same time form a small, very incomplete bibliography for those readers who want to become more familiar with Barth's life and works.

From the Protestant side:

G. C. Berkouwer, *The Triumph of Grace in the Theology of Karl Barth* (Grand Rapids, 1956); O. Weber, *Karl Barth's Church Dogmatics* (Philadelphia, 1953).

From the Catholic side:

J. Hamer, *Karl Barth* (Westminster, Maryland, 1962); H. Küng, *Justification* (Camden, New Jersey, 1964).

1

Under the Spell
of Liberalism

Karl Barth was born at Basel, Switzerland, on May 10, 1886. Three years later, the family moved to Bern, where his father, Fritz Barth, became a private teacher and later professor of Church History and New Testament Exegesis. Karl Barth's two brothers, Peter and Heinrich, were also born in the Swiss capital. The latter is at present, as was Karl until his retirement in 1962, professor at the University of Basel, where he teaches Ancient Philosophy. Although he himself has already become an important writer in his own right—namely, about Plato—still his fame has always developed in his eldest brother's shadow. Henri Bouillard, who in his description

of Karl Barth's development has unpublished biographical notes at his disposal—and from whom we
will borrow some biographical data—remarks that as
a college student Barth had an outspoken dislike for
natural sciences and mathematics. In 1904 he began
his theological studies at the University of Bern where
he attended his father's lectures. Following the German custom, he did not restrict himself to one
university, but visited various theological schools
during the years 1904-1909. From Bern he went to
Berlin. This choice was a compromise between father
and son. Karl Barth himself really wanted to go to
Marburg in order to attend Wilhelm Herrmann's
lectures, but his father objected to sending him into
such an outspoken liberal camp. He preferred Halle.
The apparently perennial conflict between the older
and the younger generation ended in this case in
amicable settlement, although one may get the impression that in the end Karl Barth got his wish a little
more than his father suspected.

Eventually, Berlin was chosen because this University, in the eyes of Fritz Barth, had neither an outspoken liberal character nor a pronounced orthodox
one. However, Karl could be well satisfied. In Berlin
there were such famous professors as Karl Holl for
Church History, Kaftan for Philosophy of Religion,
Gunkel for Exegesis and especially Adolf von Harnack. The brilliant seminars of the latter on the History of the Early Church were followed by Karl Barth
with mounting enthusiasm.

Harnack's attempt to reconcile religion and culture
made a deep impression on the young Barth, to such
an extent that he completely neglected the rich cultural
opportunities that Berlin offered outside the Univer-

sity. In a kind of intoxication he was lying chained to the feet of the great Harnack, so that even the famous Berlin Philharmonic could not entice him away from his studies. Only much later was Barth to discover that in this theology not really God but man stood in the center (KD, vol. I, 2, p. 404).* By his historical research Harnack attempted to thaw the frozen Christian dogmas, and thus ultimately to gain insight into the personality of Jesus as teacher of the true love for man.

In spite of these later discoveries Barth nonetheless has always retained an outspoken human sympathy for his great Berlin master. Years later, when people were to try to find in Harnack's writings traces of the Nazi ideology to which Germany was drifting, Karl Barth would defend him determinately with the unexpected remark: "Harnack would sooner have become a Capuchin than to join that brand of people's orators of the twenties" (KD, vol. III, 4, p. 347). Harnack was an aristocrat of the spirit and a learned man with a very high concept of the irreplaceable value of every human person.

Theologically his system was defective, but it was obvious that the Berlin students were caught under the spell of this sympathetic humanism. It is moreover a well-known phenomenon that students are usually more impressed by the human qualities of their professor than by the truths that he holds. Perhaps they unconsciously demonstrate by this that truth has aspects that have to be interpreted in the light of human values if it is not to be diminished.

* Translator's Note: The abbreviation KD throughout the text refers to Barth's *Kirchliche Dogmatik,* and all page references to Barth's works belong to the German editions.

Barth's later violent opposition against liberal theology is also partly explained by the fact that initially he himself lived consciously in this current. The *Turmerlebnis* (*Ivory Tower* experience), which is the basis of Barth's commentary on the Epistle to the Romans (*Römerbrief*) revealed to him not only the real nature of imaginary, faraway adversaries, but also that of the liberal theologian he had become during his years as a student.

Karl Barth's enthusiasm apparently had not escaped his father. It is not clear whether his stories about Harnack may have somewhat worried Barth's father. However, it is certain that at the express request of his father, Karl spent one winter term at Tübingen with Adolf Schlatter. This parental triumph did not last long, because Schlatter's exegesis was too conservative for him. At last, in the summer of 1908, he got permission to go to Marburg. There, together with the prominent professors of Philosophy, Cohen and Natorp, he found Wilhelm Herrmann at the theological faculty. Heinrich Barth, who also came to Marburg several years later, was especially impressed by the neo-Kantianism of the two famous philosophers, who have permanently influenced the trend of his philosophical thought.

Karl also attended the classes of Cohen and Natorp, but he was much more interested in Herrmann. The latter's liberal theology, which moved more in the field of ethics than of dogmatics, was inspired by Schleiermacher and Ritschl to a great extent.

This had a powerful impact on Karl Barth, who at Bern had already read Kant's *Kritik der praktischen Vernunft* (*Critique of Practical Reason*) and called this work *the* discovery of his years as a student at

Bern. Herrmann became the big idol of the young Barth who between 1908 and 1909 spent three terms at Marburg and referred to this period as the most beautiful years of his life as a student.

"Herrmann was *the* theological teacher of my student years." One may grasp something of the aura surrounding Herrmann from the characterization that was once given of him as "the most pious liberal theologian of his generation". The inspiration gained from Herrmann would later lead Barth into an altogether different direction. He himself once wrote about this: "What it means exactly to be a true disciple of a real master is a thing about which the learned men as yet do not agree. For me it means that I have let Herrmann tell me something fundamental. When I followed this fundamental idea to its conclusion, I was forced to say nearly everything else in a different way from that of Herrmann. Ultimately I was forced to understand even this fundamental idea in a different way than he had. But nevertheless, *he* had shown it to me."

The basic intuition about the absolute transcendence of God and the impossibility to provide a strictly scientific proof of God's existence were already present in Herrmann. With insistence he defended the idea that faith legitimizes itself and has no need of other sciences. Barth soon welcomed these propositions of Herrmann as the "rat poison for all the subtleties in theology".

The whole of Herrmann's theology, however, was still completely under the spell of Schleiermacher's experiential religious sense. Karl Barth would write about this later, when he had developed his own fundamental vision clearly: "Herrmann on paper, of course, contradicts me. But there is after all a Herrmann in heaven also, who perhaps does not contradict me." The polarity in Herrmann's thinking is perhaps finally best illustrated by the fact that not only Karl Barth, but also Rudolf Bultmann could look upon him as his celebrated master.

It was at Marburg that Barth also met for the first time Eduard Thurneysen, who from then on was to remain Barth's faithful comrade in arms during all his turbulent, trying times. When Karl Barth became a minister in the Canton of Aargau, in the small farm village of Safenwil, which was just then first experiencing the problems of industrialization, Thurneysen was his colleague in neighboring Leutwil. Before he occupied this post, however, Barth was for two years minister of the German Reformed community at Geneva. There he became very seriously absorbed in Calvin, but the liberal trend of his thinking, assumed in Berlin and Marburg, did not as yet undergo any change. Side by side with Calvin, his favorite remained Schleiermacher.

In 1911 he left for Safenwil. Surrounded by the massive range of the Jura mountains, hidden in one of those Swiss valleys where the sun can only rise above the mountains for a few hours a day, Barth naturally sought contact with his fellow minister at Leutwil. Thurneysen wrote about this: "Our villages were separated from each other by a few hills and valleys. We did indeed visit one another continually, but this was not enough for us. We felt an enormous need for an exchange of ideas in brotherly spirit about everything—as we then expressed it—that was taking place in the Church, the world and the kingdom of God. And because in those days there was no telephone in our rectories—something that was not entirely a disadvantage—we began a lively correspondence that was conducted almost weekly." Against the background of a friendship grown strong in this way over those years, the simple dedication that Barth wrote in 1948 in the second part of the third volume of his *Kirchliche Dogmatik* becomes more meaningful: "To Eduard Thurneysen. May your old age be like your youth!" Later on, Barth and Thurneysen, were also faithful colleagues at Basel, where the latter taught Pastoral Theology.

During the years at Safenwil, from 1911 to 1921, Karl Barth was a tireless pastor of souls. He had entertained no aspirations for a teaching post, and at first had only cultivated theology as a preparation for the sermon. For the rest of the time the pastor plunged into the social question that through industrialization was becoming highly acute in the mountain village.

In 1915 Barth became concerned about the fate of the workers and joined the Social Democratic Party. In imitation of Hermann Kutter he was of the opinion that this political society was the God-willed instrument to realize God's kingdom on earth.

He wrote to Thurneysen on this subject: "I have joined the Social Democrats. Just because Sunday after Sunday I try to preach on eschatology, I could no longer bring myself to float personally in a mist above the present wicked world. Right now it had to be made clear that faith in the most elevated things does not exclude but rather includes the sufferings and labors within the imperfections of this world. The socialists in my parish community, I hope, will understand me better now. And as for myself also, I hope now that I will no longer be unfaithful to my real orientation, something that might have happended to me two years ago in taking such a step . . . ."

The ideas by which Barth felt drawn to the religiously colored form of socialism remind one somewhat of Henriette Roland Holst van der Schalk (Dutch poetess and socialist during the turn of the century). Just like the poetess of *De vrouw in het woud* (The Woman in the Forest), Barth also soon became disillusioned. After the war, the vital, idealistic form of socialism lost his sympathy when it became clear that it could not after all withdraw from a war-mongering ideology. The eschatological meaning of the "kingdom of God" in Holy Scripture began to dawn more and more on Barth. Under the influence of the Blumhardts, father and son, he came to the conviction that Christian hope in the absolutely transcendental God had to conquer the very short-term earthly expectations of socialism. In this spirit he then wrote to Thurneysen that the political and ecclesiastical affairs really ought to be left to others. The Church must become more a real Christian community in faith and hope, and no longer an extension of the apparatus of the State.

Therefore he increasingly felt that the union between Church and State was ominous. Church and Christianity appeared far too much earth-directed, and gradually Barth began to realize that the situation was not much better with the real (liberal) theology.

2

Farewell to
Schleiermacher

Thus out of practical necessity arose the need to take his place once more behind the study desk. Barth wanted to test his growing vision on the Bible. In collaboration with Thurneysen he began a work that was originally not meant for publication but only for an intimate circle of friends, in order to infuse genuine Christian life into preaching. He could not do otherwise. The meaning of human existence had to be studied anew in a Christian spirit. A few overly worried people looked upon this as a rather risky undertaking. Barth's mental health might suffer by it. Not without some irony he told Thurneysen in a letter: "I have put on my glasses once more, after those beautiful days in Bern. I am preparing a lecture, and as always I find it hard again. Our psychonanalytical house-mate at Bern told me that I should not worry so much about the meaning of this life. It affects my health and would never let me find rest. According to him I ought to take up some interest or other (temperance or something like that) to spend my energy on. That would be of more practical use for both myself and others. If only that were really possible! To put one's teeth firmly into something, to run along enthusiastically with something with the triumphant cry that this is it! Instead, my dominant feeling is one of nostalgic desire to show myself and others what life is really all about. That is why I cannot even rouse enough naiveté in myself to patch together a touching little sermon or talk."

Barth then began to work at a thorough exegesis of Paul's Epistle to the Romans. A new world, although an unexpected one, opened up for him.

As is often the case, the theologian Barth found that the dutiful explanations of the exegete only rarely supplied him with any light. They were too little theologically interested. Only J. T. Beck could meet with his approval: ". . . simply towering above the rest of the company!"

Progress of the work was extremely slow. Thurneysen received regular progress reports. On September 1, 1916, one said: "I am wrestling at present with the massive mountain of Romans 3, 20, and following verses. What a wealth of meaning is hidden behind all this! With this first assault I can hardly discover and digest it all. It more or less concerns the same things we met in the First Epistle of John, only more pointedly; if you wish, more dangerously." Finally, when the work was completed it was published after all in 1919, contrary to his original intention. The great central rediscovery, by which Barth was going to turn away definitively from liberal theology, did not show itself markedly as yet in this first edition. This really took place only in the second and completely revised edition that appeared in 1922. But meanwhile, the first edition had caused quite a sensation and shattered a couple of theological glass houses. Later, in the Introduction to the first part of his *Christliche Dogmatik* (*Christian Dogmatics in Outline*), Barth wrote about this: "When I am looking back on my life I see myself as someone who gropes his way up a dark bell tower, and who in doing so, without in the least suspecting it, instead of the handrail, grabs a rope that proves to be the bell rope. Much to his own consternation he suddenly hears the bell begin to ring—and really not for himself alone. What can he do, other than climb on as carefully as possible?"

The bell rang for many people. Upon a single sound of it Barth had become famous. The beginning of 1921 showed that also in Germany people had heard the ringing sound.

The request that reached him then was to determine the outward course of his life. How diffidently he himself reacted to this is shown in the following quotation from a letter of February 1, 1921: "An enormous rock has fallen in the quiet pond here: from Göttingen I got the message that the Reformed community there (as it seems to me with the approval of the faculty) want me for a chair of Systematic Theology that they hope to erect and pay for with funds from America!

"On February 7, when Minister Haenisch is coming

to Göttingen, I have to give a reply, which will not be binding for the time being. What I would most like to do would be to take the first train to St. Gallen in order to assess this damage with you [Thurneysen]: Professor, Systematic Theology, Göttingen, Hannover, Germany, all question marks. In the background, America (the Western World)—a big question mark."

Astonishment, irony and serious objections to certain aspects of the future that probably awaited him in Germany were outlined in this letter. Nevertheless he accepted the offer and in October 1921 left for Göttingen where he began to publish in cooperation with Paul Tillich and Rudolf Bultmann. Shortly after his arrival he received a message of sympathy from Münster in Westphalia, where he was to move in 1925 as regular lecturer in Dogmatics.

"Just now the mail brings me the sensational news that I am being offered an honorary doctorate in Dogmatic Theology from Münster 'for real contributions to a more profound statement of religious and theological problems'. In heaven—at least in the corner where the opposition meets—this honor will probably have caused a mild surprise. On earth this afternoon a simple cup of black coffee . . ."

Meanwhile the second edition of the *Römerbrief* had been completed, in which Barth with prophetical seriousness passed his verdict on liberal theology. The liberals had injured God's transcendency, and therefore also the faith, in their attempt to render this popular with the aid of religious science, the historical method and philosophy.

The infinite qualitative distinction between God and creature, eternity and time, kingdom of God and the world had been reasoned away, and hence faith was no longer a risky leap in the dark. Barth argued against this that faith is a miracle of God's vertical and punctual intervention in man's life, without this intervention ever becoming the kind of reality that can be localized, and takes place within this world.

To a bewildering extent Barth saw that this very vision was the basic inspiration for Matthias Grünewald's famous Isenheim altar. Mary as well as John the Baptist stand in the darkness of the faith. "Only the Infant Himself, not the Mother, sees what is to be seen there (on the right-hand side): the Father; just as only the Father is looking the Child in the eyes" (KD, vol. I, 2, p. 137). Mary can only pray believing, John the Baptist can only point. In this way they are prototypes of the Church which, fully aware of God's impalpable transcendency, can only point upward from the darkness.

God is the totally Other One, and our surrender to Him in the faith has all the paradoxical and unreasoned qualities of an existential giving away of oneself. "Christianity" as an institutionalized reality is a monstrosity; only the Christian who here and now risks himself for this most sublimely individual existence is real before God. Revelation is not an idea, not a publication of eternal truths, but a breathtaking event in which God continuously gives Himself to be known and loved. Within the context of this return to the biblical notion of faith, which Barth thought he had rediscovered in Paul, it becomes understandable that elsewhere, also against every liberalistic tendency, he formulated the famous pronouncement: "I consider the *analogia entis* as an invention of the antichrist and I think that for this reason alone one cannot become a Catholic. While

at the same time I permit myself to look upon all
the other reasons one may have for not becoming a
Catholic as shortsighted and not to be taken seriously."

It is clear what is essential here for Barth. Still
in this rather negative period he wanted to point out
clearly that God, revelation and faith are not worldly
entities, as liberal theology often suggested, and also
as—according to Barth—the First Vatican Council
meant in its defense of the natural knowledge of
God, but something *sui generis*. Faith is no longer
faith at the very moment when one looks for a support, some guarantee within this world, on the
strength of which it would be reasonable to believe.
From this world there is no possibility to rise up to
God; the movement takes place in exactly the oppo-
site way: it is only through faith that this world
becomes a reality. Several Protestant theologians
recognized in this vision of Barth's an old patrimony
from the Reformation. People of the same mind seek
one another, so that soon we can speak of a group,
to which not only Thurneysen, but also Gogarten,
Brunner and Rudolf Bultmann belonged. It may
perhaps come as a surprise to find this last name also
in this neo-orthodox company. Due to the rather
sensational interest in some details of Bultmann's
program of demythologizing in recent years, many
will want to count him among the ultraliberal
theologians. But this is not correct. Bultmann's
fundamental intitution is very close to Barth's. Both
want to detach the act of faith again from historical,
earthly certainties; both have brought the act of faith
into connection with man's actual existential giving

away of self, by which he renounces the search for objective guarantees in verifiable history. In the elaboration of this fundamental principle, Barth and Bultmann have eventually followed different paths, but the point of departure of both lies unmistakably in a common defensive attitude toward liberal theology.

Barth's point of departure was therefore biblical, if with some "prophetic" overtones. Still also the philosophy of existence, as he had come to know it in Kierkegaard, originally played a very big part. In his Preface to the revised edition of the *Römerbrief* Barth tells his readers that the only system he knows is Kierkegaard's, formulated in the adage of the infinite qualitative distinction between time and eternity. Two years later, he still called the Danish philosopher "the greatest Christian thinker of the last century". Barth felt kinship with the tormented Kierkegaard, who had spoken in open rebellion against the secularized Established Church. In him he found the paradoxical situation of human existence before God described in all force. Barth quoted Kierkegaard with violent agreement when the latter chose to look upon Christianity as a scandal: "If one takes away the possibility of scandal, as one has done in Christianity, the whole Christian faith is reduced to direct revelation, and then the whole of Christianity has been abolished. It has become something easy and superficial that can neither wound somebody deeply nor heal him; it then becomes the untruthful invention of purely human sympathy, in which the infinite qualitative distinction between God and man is forgotten" (*Römerbrief*, second edition, p. 73).

During his professorship at Münster and Bonn, however, Barth began to separate himself more and more from Kierkegaard. The notion of "existence", borrowed from Kierkegaard, gradually disappeared from his vocabulary, because ultimately Barth feared, not without reason, that with it he was still bringing a chunk of philosophy or psychology within the city-walls of his theology. According to Barth, it was through this Trojan horse that Bultmann fell.

In 1932, when Barth was in Bonn, the first part of his main work, *Kirchliche Dogmatik,* appeared, four parts of which in the meanwhile have been published in twelve volumes. In the first edition of this first part, "existential thinking" in theology is already called a remnant of pietism. In the third edition of 1945, the notion of existence is exclusively relegated to ethics. When in 1947 Barth published his Bonn lectures on "Die protestantische Theologie im 19 Jahrhundert" (Protestant Theology in the 19th Century), he no longer thought it necessary even to mention Kierkegaard's name.

In the end, Barth even began to take offense at Kierkegaard's sharp attacks. The case of Bishop Mynster is symptomatic of this. The Danish philosopher saw established Christianity, comfortably settled in the world, embodied in the unquestionable respect that this Bishop enjoyed among his coreligionists. That is why this Bishop became the brunt of Kierkegaard's definitely harsh criticism. In later years Barth wondered with regard to this episode whether a bishop really should be attacked only "because he was a generally respected bishop?" (KD, vol. III, 4, p. 773)

One might argue that Barth had gradually mellowed through his experience of life. His ruthless

criticism had softened, or—to quote his own words—
the lion had lost some of his teeth in the heat of the
fight and now had to start eating grass. It is, however,
not only a matter of mature wisdom, let alone a diminished aggressiveness. By his later confrontation with
Bultmann and the latter's success, Barth began to fear
the fatal consequences that, according to him, existentialism produced in theology. The more fashionable
it became to appeal to Kierkegaard, the less Barth felt
inclined to rely on him as a philospher. He considered
it necessary to take the objective elements in theology
—Trinity, predestination, christology—clearly under
his protection against this new fashion (KD, vol. IV,
3, p. 573). Finally, some years ago we heard Barth
speak entirely in general and not very flatteringly about
"those horrible Danes", who could only think in terms
of capricious contrasts.

This development is not surprising. Indeed, with the
notion of existence, Barth too ran the risk of bringing
the whole inventory of liberal theology within the walls
once more. By way of this detour, which in the beginning might seem without danger, subjectivism and
psychologism would have forced their way in again
after all.

As of now it is impossible to give a definitive evalu-
ation of Bultmann's development since then, or
especially of his still faster-developing disciples. However, it may be that Barth's fear of Kierkegaard's
influence was not entirely without justification. The
"secular meaning of the Gospel" can ultimately be
stressed to such an extent that very little remains of
true revelation.

3

From Kierkegaard
to Anselm

Pure negation is a bad starting point for theology. Therefore the mere rejection of all sorts of liberal tendencies also had in the long run to be succeeded by a positive orientation. Thus we see Barth soon developing and fortifying his methodological starting point. For this purpose he consulted the first systematic Scholastic, Anslem of Canterbury. In 1931 his new work appeared: *Fides quaerens intellectum. Anselms Beweis der Existenz Gottes, in Zusammenhang seines theologischen Programms* (Faith Seeking Intellect. Anselm's Proof of the Existence of God, in the Context of His Theological Program).

Only recently have we begun to see that this work is extremely important for the understanding of Barth's theological method. That this realization came late indeed appears among other things from the fact that "to my sad surprise"—as Barth wrote—it was not until 1958 that a second edition of this work on Anselm followed. In the Preface to this second edition Barth said that only a few—among whom Hans Urs von Balthasar is mentioned by name—understood that it is not out of pure love for history that he has turned to Anselm. "It has escaped most people that this book on Anselm is, if not the only one, at least a very important key to understanding the trend of thought that seemed to me to be the only theologically correct one in *Kirchliche Dogmatik.*" If one interprets Anselm rationalistically, as mostly happens, this predilection of Barth's for the great early Scholastic is rather surprising. After all, was it not precisely Barth's intention to turn the spotlight on faith as an absolutely new starting point, a miracle of grace, without any rationalistic gateways? Indeed, he remained faithful to this plan; how could he do otherwise? Barth considered, therefore, all of Anselm's so-called "natural" arguments for the existence and essence of God as situated within the large circle of the surrender of faith. *Credo ut intelligam* (I believe in order that I may understand), *i.e.*, starting from the faith, the believer attempts to read the mystery *intus-legere* (from the inside). He tries to approach the theological intelligibility of the mystery by a comparison of the various data of the faith. When there is a question or *ratio* (reason), we should not understand this exclusively in the sense of the subjective, natural reason, but of the objective *ratio veritatis,* the proportion of intelligibility that is contained in the mystery itself, because every mystery of faith is a participation in the supreme truth.

This interpretation of Anselm by Barth certainly has this great advantage; namely, that it shows a clear consciousness of the fact that the medieval thinkers could be theologians, even though they worked with natural reason. It is moreover not clear how one could ever be a theologian otherwise, but it seems to be necessary to spell this out from time to time.

Barth's interpretation of Anselm has evoked quite a bit of opposition from the historians. They reproached him for searching medieval texts with a systematic preoccupation (apparently an abomination to historians!) and then forced these to provide him with an answer to a question that had not been a question for the medieval theologian, so that he really could not give an answer to it either.

Etienne Gilson, an eminent authority on the Middle Ages, has in this connection given an interesting hint to all students of systematic sciences who are concerned with historical research.*

History for those students, says Gilson, is something like a railway mail-car in which a postal clerk rides along: "All around him are pigeonholes and each carries a name: theology, philosophy, idealism, realism, pantheism, nominalism, with all their divisions and subdivisions. Just as the postal clerk knows that there is a pigeonhole for every letter, so the historian knows that there is a separate box for every doctrine. His only problem is to read the envelopes

* Cf. Etienne Gilson, "Sens et nature de l'argument de Saint Anselm," in *Arch. d'hist. doctr. et litt. du MA* 9 (1934) 43.

and distribute the letters in accordance with their addresses. . . . But why should we—instead of sorting out the doctrines in the prearranged holes—not rather ask history which pigeonholes we ought to set up in the mail-car, in order to put the doctrines we find into them? . . . The method of the pigeonholes is the method of philosophy when it enters the field of history. . . . True historical research, however, always deals with particulars. It always considers this particular philosophy, this particular theology or this particular mysticism."

Gilson's general conclusion is that it is very dangerous to search history for the confirmation of one's preconceived opinions. That is why he rejects Barth's interpretation of Anselm. For Anselm the problem "philosophy" or "theology" did not exist. Even the word theology hardly ever occurs in his writings. With all due respect for Barth's meticulous research and his opinion that Anselm could not work otherwise than as a faithful medieval believer, it would still be an anachronism to search in his work for some scorn of the relative autonomy of human reason (and of course to find it). Here also the principle holds: he who proves too much, proves nothing.

This devastating argument of Gilson contains a memorable warning and at the same time a qualification of Barth's judgment on Anselm. However, one would like to see Gilson's critical observations completed by a word of praise for the systematic Barth who was not afraid to take upon himself the tiresome work of an historian. Professional historians are often so marvelously objective in their task that one wonders after all their reseach if they have actually come to any real conclusions. The temptation then becomes great for the systematist—and this, too, history can prove only too well, unfortunately—to build up speculations in empty space, void of historical fact.

It was definitely not without some justification that Barth found in Anselm both an inspiration and a confirmation for his theological method. The reflection of the believer does not take place solely from below to above; not by ascending from natural evidence to the heavenly mysteries. At the beginning of all theology there is the descent of God, who revealed Himself to men. That Barth took this opportunity in passing, also to condemn natural theology may seem to us to be going a little too far, but this should not cause us to loose sight of what has real value in his vision. The direction from below to above—from the earthly to the divine mysteries—is for Barth the abominable road of the *analogia entis* (analogy of being). The other road, from above to below, is that of the *analogia fidei* (analogy of faith); descending from faith, the Christian acquires an insight into the Christian truths. It is possible to juxtapose these two forms of analogy in less sharp contrast. Inside the analogy of faith the analogy of being must have its place. If it did not, then God's self-revelation would be—according to an expression of Brunner's in a polemic with Barth—a "dangerous Chinese business". If the revelation is to be comprehensible for us humans, then the terminolgy of the Christian mysteries of salvation must be related to the data of experience of the world in which we live.

One year after the appearance of Barth's study on Anselm, the first part of his *Kirchliche Dogmatik* was published. During the first years of his professorship at Göttingen, he had not yet felt any need to write a new systematic course of dogma. In 1924, when he had to give a complete course in dogmatic theology for the first time, he reached back to a work by Heppe published in 1861. There he learned how very necessary it is for a theologian to keep in touch with the Christian heritage. In a certain sense every theologian has to make a fresh start, but on the other hand, every fresh start means a critical integration of what others have studied before. Therefore in 1927 the first part of Barth's *Christliche Dogmatik* was published but was then completely revised and introduced in 1932 as a new book, the first part of his *Kirchliche Dogmatik*. The confrontation with Anslem, which took place between the publications of the *Christliche Dogmatik* and the *Kirchliche Dogmatik,* has left its traces. Already the change of title reflected Barth's new view on the specific nature of theology. The real exercise of theology can only take place within the field of the Church and in the service of the Church. Moreover, only there may one speak of a real "Christianity", although according to Barth one might well make a more sparing use of this big word.

In his *Christliche Dogmatik* the Word of God was also still proposed as the answer to the questions that human existence on this earth necessarily presents. Man finds that he lives on earth as a stranger, deprived of God and in enmity with his neighbor. And all this through his own guilt. To this guilt God's Word provides the answer. It saves man in the expectation of a better future. Precisely in this answer man becomes fully conscious of his sinfulness. Especially in order to emphasize this last point, and thus avoid the appearance that a philosophical analysis of human existence alone would suffice to convince man of his sinfulness and need for redemption, the whole setup in the *Christliche Dogmatik* was changed. The Word of God was no longer presented as the answer to the problem of man's existence. Actually, the possibility of "deducting" certain dimensions of the Word of God from a phenomenological analysis of human existence had not been excluded. Barth readily admitted that by his methodology in the *Christliche Dogmatik* he had given rise to this misunderstanding: "An anthropology—even a religious anthropology—would have defined the origin of our knowledge about the crucial elements of the Word of God exactly like that. So at that time I did pay my toll to the idols after all" (KD, vol. I. 1, p.130). In the *Kirchliche Dogmatik* he bids consistent farewell to every form of philosophical existentialism as relevant to theology. In line with this rejection of every form of philosophy he also takes a clear stand against a "natural theology".

Barth's ideas became much more crystallized. His farewell to Kierkegaard is more clearly pronounced. He learned how to perceive more keenly the danger of "anthropologizing" theology: "One can even ask himself seriously whether this anthropologizing does not also take place in what is being promoted today—in conjunction with Kierkegaard, but still consciously or unconsciously as a continuation of the pietistic tradition—as 'existential' theological thinking and speaking." Anselm, and with him several other Christian thinkers of the age of high Scholasticism, put their mark on the further development of the *Kirchliche Dogmatik*. The serious study that Barth made of these personalities again supplied new food for the ever present "alarmed" critics. They warned him that he was "historically, formally and materially on the road

of Scholasticism". They went still further in their
objections to Barth: for him Church History apparently did not begin with the year 1517; he was not
reluctant to quote Anselm and Thomas; in one way
or other he still considered the old Church's dogma
as normative: he still continued to defend extensively
a doctrine of the Trinity, and even the doctrine of the
virgin birth. This last point especially seemed to many
an extremely dubious sign. Barth asked himself what
he would answer to this litany of sighs: "Am I perhaps
doing the right thing by pointing out that the coherence
between the Reformation and the old Church, the
trinitarian and christological dogma, the notion of
dogma in general and even the idea of a biblical canon
are after all not just my own wicked inventions?"
(KD, vol. I, 1, p.ix)

In the great medieval theologians Barth also found
the "flavor" of genuine theology. They knew that
theology claims the whole man. Anselm had also
confirmed this with his life. Born in Italy, he had after
a stormy youth roamed all over France in order to
land finally, by accident, as it were, in a Benedictine
abbey. There he was struck by the stature of the monk
Lanfranc who received him and who soon created
the background that enabled the restless Anselm to
become the first systematic theologian of the Middle
Ages. With such a background his theology could
not be just a routine branch of study. A century later,
Abelard, also dubbed as a rationalist, would demonstrate the same thing. Barth sensed this and it was
one of the reasons that he felt attracted to Anselm. In
the first chapter of Anselm's knife-sharp *Proslogion*
(an ontological proof of the existence of God) he
had read this untranslatable adomonition: "Oh, weak

man, do withdraw from your busy occupations, throw
off your pressing worries and let go your interior
dividedness. . . . Make yourself a little free for God
and find some rest in Him. 'Enter into the inner
chamber' of your heart, lock everything else out except
God and what may help you to find Him, and 'when
you have locked the door' then seek Him. Say now
with all your heart, say to God: 'My face hath sought
thee: thy face, O Lord, will I still seek'."

From this monk who had scarcely found rest and
wrote down these words, Barth also learned that the
study of theology is not exclusively a "useful" occupation that prepares spiritual consumer goods for the
benefits of preachers and clericalizing laymen. To be
dissolved in God is something of a supreme beauty.
With full agreement Barth quoted Anselm where the
latter called the understanding born of the faith, of
the coherence of the works of God's revelation "beautiful beyond all human understanding". One can enjoy
it (*delectari*), the abbot of Bec mused. Barth took
over these musings and said: "It may well be pointed
out for once that theology is a science of exceptional
beauty. One may even safely say that among all
sciences she is the most beautiful of all. It is always
a sign of barbarism when science bores somebody. But
what a double barbarism it is when theology bores
somebody or could possibly bore him. One can only
happily and joyfully be a theologian, or he is none at
all. Sour faces, sad thoughts and boring talk are especially intolerable in the branch of learning. May God
preserve us from what Catholic theology points out as
one of the seven sins of a monk: the *taedium,* an
interior repugnance concerning the great spiritual
truths that theology deals with. We must fully real-

ize, however, that only God can preserve us from this" (KD, vol. II, 1, p.740).

Theology therefore, if it must be practiced well, requires man's full life. Barth noticed this in the great medieval theologians and he has also put it into practice himself. However, he did not want any misunderstandings. There might be the danger that one would stress the closeness to life and the existential character of theology in such a way as imperceptibly to emerge again in the immediate vicinity of Schleiermacher's theology of experience or of Zinzendorf's pietism.

Barth therefore put it more precisely: at all times the self-revealing God must remain at the center. Whether man cries out with a loud voice that he is succumbing under God's weight—as St. Christopher once did—may perhaps be pathetic or even interesting, but theologically it is unimportant. It would be a degeneration of theology if it were degraded to some "news report on the human situation (radically revealed in the faith) by the here-and-now speaking theologian".

In theology, Barth once said, there should not be too much "Kierkegaarding". Anselm showed him the golden mean. For this medieval theologian it would have come as a small but not disagreeable surprise that Barth quoted him in the same breath with Luther and Melanchthon. After all, one can learn from them that theology is not "some objectless contemplative science outside the Church". It is because the true theologians fully realized this that they also prayed, Barth affirmed. They did this with all the more reason precisely because they would all the better begin to realize the fragility of their work. "It was not some monkish stylistic exercise when Anselm spoke about the *imbecillitas scientiae meae,* the foolishness of my theological knowledge."

Wherever a man thinks profoundly about the mystery of God, there every form of human pride disappears. Thomas Aquinas is also an eloquent proof of this for Barth. With some relish Barth wrote of him: "It is said of Thomas Aquinas, whose *Summa Theologica,* as is well-known, has remained a torso, that to a request to continue his writing he answered: 'Reginald, I can no longer do it, because all that I have written seems to me like straw. I hope that God will soon put an end to my writing and teaching.' Against this another episode does not seem to matter much. Just when he was busy with the christological part of his work, Christ would have appeared to him with the words: 'You have written well about me, Thomas!' The doctor of the Church who wears a halo, however, has been relegated by Thomas himself to the realm of eschatology" (KD, vol. I, 1, p.21). It is not impossible that Barth's work will also remain a torso. . . .

4

Barth and
Politics

While at Bonn, from 1934 to 1935, Karl Barth
entered into open conflict with the Nazi regime. Compromise never agreed with him in any field, so that it
is not surprising that things came to a clear break.
Nevertheless the number of years that now separate
us from those events must not let us forget that it took
a rather sharp faculty of discernment and great moral
courage to resist the regime in those days. Several
theologians and Church dignitaries did not recognize
the dangers of National Socialism early enough. That
this was not only the case within the Protestant
Churches has been shown in a fiercely debated article

in the German magazine *Hochland*.* Well-known
theologians and Church dignitaries exerted themselves
in those dark years to build a bridge of understanding
between Catholicism and National Socialism. It is
not very encouraging for theology to see what high
principles proved to be open to multiple interpretation
in the process. Protestantism with its twenty-eight
State Churches was in 1933, if possible, even more
vulnerable. The National Socialistic leaders attempted
to unite them into one national Church under the
leadership of Hitler's favorite protégé Ludwig Müller.
This movement seemed to catch on with many
"German Christians", until the time when Müller
began to separate himself too clearly from the evangelical principles. As a Swiss, Barth followed the
good fortune and woe of the Church with keen objective interest. In November 1933 the Bonn professor of
Theology thought that the time had come to go into
action.

A synod was convened at Barmen, for which Barth
wrote the minutes that were later revised by Hans
Asmussen and Thomas Breit. With an unusual solem-
nity, which this time did not lack in clarity, the first
"Barmen-thesis" quoted the words of John 14, 6:
"I am the way, the truth and the life; no man cometh
to the Father, but by me." Consequently, the error
was rejected "that the Church would have to accept
as a source of her teaching—beyond and besides the
one and only Word of God—any other events and
powers, forms and truths as God's revelation".

Later, Hans Asmussen wrote about this: "This

* Cf. E. W. Böckenförde, "Der deutsche Katholizismus
im Jahre 1933," in *Hochland* 53 (1961), 215-239. For reply
and rejoinder cf. *ibid.*, 497-515, and 54 (1962), 217-245.

statement is perhaps the loftiest that has ever been
enunciated on the whole Church-State struggle. It
almost entirely originated from Barth. I consider it of
such great value for the reason that in it the great
question of the Church struggle has been reduced
to an act of witness for or against Christ." Although
many former friends could not justify Barth's attitude
—in 1933 he saw himself obliged to turn his back on
his collaborator of the first hour, Friedrich Gogarten—
still he could not retreat one step. As a free Swiss he
remained inflexible. That is why an open rupture
became inevitable. No absolutist system can tolerate
continuous opposition in its midst. Exactly a year
later, November of 1934 ,came the climax of the crisis.

The fact that Karl Barth did not open his lectures
with the Nazi salute, as had been ordered, proved the
first occasion of friction. As ordinary professor of
Theology he was further obliged to take an oath of
fidelity to Hitler. He declared, however, that he would
only be prepared to do this when the clause was added:
"insofar as I can justify this as an evangelical Christian". On November 27, 1934, his students came to
the classroom in vain. Miss von Kirschbaum, who
was Barth's secretary at the time, had to tell them that
Karl Barth had been removed from office for his
refusal to take the oath of allegiance. After a fruitless
attempt to get Barth to come to the Netherlands, he
left for Switzerland, where at Basel he became a fellow
professor of K. L. Schmidt, Oscar Cullman, Thurneysen and others. When he returned to Bonn after the
war to become a guest-lecturer, he wrote to one of
his former students: "With regard to Germany, I am
more or less in the position of Gretchen: he loves
me . . . he loves me not . . . loves me . . ."

Looking back on this stormy period it must be stated
that Barth's struggle, at least initially, was not at
bottom against National Socialism as a political power.
His attack was primarily directed against the confusion to which the "German Christians" had fallen
prey. They hailed in the new system a kind of divine
revelation and in this way sinned against the first
commandment of the decalogue. Insofar as National
Socialism as a totalitarian system was the occasion for
this, Barth evidently also opposed this system. In the
dramatic months before Chamberlain flew to Munich
to discuss with Hitler his claims to Czechoslovakia,
Barth published his famous letter to Hromádka, professor at Prague. It was Monday, September 19, 1938,
around noon. At that moment Barth still did not
know whether England and France would give in to
Hitler through the British Prime Minister: "Do they
realize that today—insofar as we humans can judge
this—the liberty of the whole of Europe, and maybe
not only that of Europe, depends on the liberty of
your people? . . ." And if it should come to the point
that Chamberlain might give in: "Will your government and your people then—and only then—really
stand in the breach for liberty? It is very clear to me
what misery you are calling upon yourselves by this.
Still I dare hope that the sons of the old Hussites will
show weakened Europe that even today there are still
real men. Every Czech soldier who will fight or suffer
will do this also for us. Today I even make bold to
add without any reservation: he will do it also for the
Church of Jesus Christ, which in the atmosphere of a
Hitler or a Mussolini can only collapse in ridicule or
total downfall. What a strange time, dear colleague,
in which a reasonable man can only say one thing,

namely, that faith commands us to put resolutely in second place the fear of violence and the love of peace, and just as resolutely to put in first place the fear of injustice and the love of freedom."

Not only in Germany, but also in Holland, this letter caused much sensation. Was it possible to identify the national liberty of the Czech State so directly with the liberty of the Church? Had all the contemplations about the transcendency and the eschatological meaning of the kingdom of God suddenly become powerless under pressure of political circumstances? In the same year, 1938, Barth had already occupied himself more systematically with these problems. In the spring he had been invited by Aberdeen University to give the Gifford Lectures there. It was indeed a great honor for him, but not without a certain savory connotation. Lord Gifford, who died in 1887, had stipulated in his last will that from the inheritance an annual series of lectures were to be financed that would serve to promote natural theology. That precisely the traditional enemy of the *analogia entis* was now invited naturally caused some complications. In spite of Barth's objections to the formulation of the theme, the invitation was maintained. Barth then restricted himself to an elaborate explanation of the Scottish Presbyterian confession. In this connection he devoted a lecture to the twenty-fourth article of this written confession, under the title "politischer Gottesdienst" (Political Religion). He rejected in this absolute separation of Church and State and propounded as his opinion that under certain circumstances it might become a Christian duty to oppose a State that wanted to oppress the Church and idolatrously place itself in the center of interest.

A few months later, Barth developed his ideas further in a lecture on "Rechtfertigung und Recht" (Justification and Right). Neither in Luther's *Von weltlicher Obrigkeit* (On Secular Authority), nor Calvin's *Institutie* (Institutes) did Barth find a satisfactory answer to the serious problems that occupied him: Do the social order, peace and liberty have a place in the sanctifying work of the Spirit? Does the redemption, which after all has been accomplished in Christ, have anything to do with human rights, so that these in some way or other hold a place within the surrender of the faith? Is there such a thing as an actively political religion? The Reformers had only written that no contradiction exists between divine and human rights. They did not get down to a positive definition, and by this, according to Barth, they had opened the way to pietism and *Aufklärung* (enlightenment).

Barth's own vision elaborated on K. L. Schmidt's inaugural address that compared power of the State to the biblical powers of the angels, which were threatened by the danger of self-exaltation. The Church is the new State of the new heaven and the new earth. The power of the secular State, biblically personified in Pilate, is in itself free, and may be used for good or for evil. Pilate could have acquitted Christ. This would have meant that one recognized Jesus' right to preach the redemption. But even in the abuse that Pilate made of his power by ordering Jesus' crucifixion. "He was the human instrument of the justification of sinful man, to be fulfilled once for all by this crucifixion." Pilate declared his solidarity with the guilt of the Jews, but through this, also, with the promises that had been made to Israel. Just like

Pilate, the demonic State can indeed want the evil, but still—in spite of itself—in order to be forced to do the good in an eminent way. The governor who condemned Christ had made this eminently clear because in spite of everything he declared emphatically that Jesus was innocent. In that moment the State showed its true essence. Insofar as this essence was contradicted by later action, the State is unfaithful to itself. The demonic State is therefore too little really a State. Having once established this, Barth emphasized that the officials of the State—also biblically— were " extraordinary ministers of the Church".

In two successive chapters Barth further indicated the task of the State with regard to the Church and the significance of the Church for the State. The Christian cannot put any absolute hope in the State, because the Christian expectation of salvation is directed toward the heavenly Jerusalem. But Barth maintained, "The heavenly city is not being erected on the ruins of the destroyed magnificence of earthly peoples and kings. All that earthly magnificence will be delivered as a tribute to the heavenly city." That is also why a complete demonizing of the State is impossible. It is the task of the Church to preach the future kingdom. In order to be able to do this in peace and freedom, the Church needs the State. On the other hand, the State cannot complete this task without the prayer of the Church.

With this Barth had already arrived at a positive formulation of the task of the Church in relation to the State. The Church must pray that the State obtain the necessary power, and this without asking herself whether the State is also prepared to return reciprocal service to the Church. As for her preaching to the

State, the Church should further remember that the suffering of injustice may sometimes be a more efficient witness than any flaming protest. If, however, the State falls into a certain form of satanic activity, then, in the nature of things, only a limited respect is possible. The Church should also give to the State certain guarantees. To these belongs the guarantee that she requires of her members the fulfillment of their civic duties. What are these duties according to Barth? The oath of allegiance? The Reformers answered this question affirmatively. It will come as no surprise that Barth—also considering his personal background—made some qualification here. The State can never require a total, unconditional oath. Does military service also belong to that which the Church should admonish her faithful members to do? Again the Reformers answered affirmatively. Barth agreed with them on this point and justified it by the thesis: "Human rights need the guarantee of human might." When the question was raised of whether the State can also oblige man interiorly to accept its philosophy of life, Barth answered in the negative with an appeal to Holy Scripture. The same Holy Scripture, however, admonishes us to pray *and* to work. On the basis of this the Church must also require political activity from her members. "The fulfillment of our political duties is not exhausted with the payment of taxes or with other passive compliances with the law," Barth affirmed.

In a later refinement of these questions it appeared that at times political struggle may also be a Christian duty. Barth, then, appealed to article fourteen of the Scottish confession, in which resistance to tyranny is mentioned. In line with this last remark Barth further specified his attitude toward National Socialism. This happened in a later publication in which the dictatorship that practiced this system was called a temptation to idolatry. Therefore the Church had to pray for the defeat of National Socialism and the revival of a just State. During the years 1939 and 1940 Barth showed himself a fervent protagonist of the right and duty to wage war against Hitler. Immediately after the war, however, he joined as fervently in the fight for the human rights of the defeated Germany. The Germans, he said, did not need moral professors at that time, but friends. Perhaps the tragedy of the German people was also in part to be explained by the fact that we had made it impossible for them to believe in solidarity and genuine friendship.

Barth's attitude toward National Socialism might lead one to expect that he would fight Russian Communism with the same vehemence founded on the same basic convictions. The idolatrous traits of excessive self-esteem have a great similarity in both systems. It is at least a proof of Barth's independent thinking that he did not automatically confirm this similarity. With increasing stubborness Barth refused to be pinned down on the historical decision he had taken with regard to National Socialism. According to him, there was a big difference between National Socialism and the Soviet ideology. In spite of everything, Russia was animated by a constructive idea that was born of a real and acute problem: the social question. The solution that was given to this problem in the so-called Free West was not the only correct one; it cannot be, as long as this freedom is abused in order to cause economic crises, to destroy grain while people die of hunger.

The atheism of Russian Communism had, at any rate, the advantage that it showed itself openly. National Socialism tried to falsify Christianity by now and then assuming a Christian appearance. And furthermore, Barth also still wondered whether Russian atheism was so very different from the factual atheism that had penetrated the West on the streets and in the newspapers.

In spite of the fact that the majority of Western theologians took up positions against Russian Communism, Barth continued to ask for understanding. He did not want to break off communications and refused to see in what happened in Russia a complete demoralizing of the State. That was why the Churches of the West had no right to take an unqualified stand against Russia. This position of Barth has indeed lent a particularly tragic note to the latter part of his life. His farewell lecture at Basel in March of 1962 could have been an apotheosis. On account of the dissensions concerning his successor, it did not become an apotheosis but a painful incident. Already for months the name of Helmut Gollwitzer had been mentioned as Barth's likely successor in teaching Dogmatics. Barth recognized and esteemed in him a sympathetic spirit, also in political matters. But precisely for this reason there arose a violent polemic against his candidacy. In reply to Barth's farewell address, which dealth with the implications of Christian charity, the Pro-Rector of Basel University delivered a remarkable speech in which he expressed political and scientific criticism of Barth's lifework. A consequence of one and the other was that not Gollwitzer, but Heinrich Ott was appointed as Barth's successor. Insofar as the latter propounds a theology that moves more in

the direction of Rudolf Bultmann, one may say
that with this not only an attempt was made to dis-
approve Barth's political ideas, but that very consciously a theological trend was chosen that was not
Karl Barth's line.

Barth's attitude with regard to Communism has
remained incomprehensible for many people. It is
therefore not surprising that in a review on the years
1948-1958 he dwelt rather long on this point. "It is
not true that I could muster some sort of sympathy for
the Communism of Eastern Europe", he declared. "I
am definitely glad that I do not have to live within the
sphere of influence of Communism and I wish that no
one be forced to do that. However, I do not see
that it would be a political, nay even a Christian duty
to attach to this antipathy the same consequences that
one has been evermore attaching to it during these
fifteen years. Anti-Communism as a principle seems
to me to be an even greater evil than Communism
itself. Can one overlook the fact that Communism is
the unwelcome, but in all its unnaturalness still the
natural consequence and the natural answer to Western developments?" According to Barth, the Western
world is equally, but more subtly, threatened by an
assault on human liberty. "Has one forgotten", he
wonders, "that only the 'Hitler' in us can be a prin-
cipled anti-Communist? . . . Who in the Western world
has taken the trouble just for once to ponder over the
painful situation that began in 1945, from the Eastern
point of view, especially the Russian one? Were
people not rather pleased—and rightly so—about the
Soviet contribution to the victory over the National
Socialistic danger? Is it not the leaders of the Western
world who toward the end of the war have permitted

and assured to the Soviet a dominating position in all forms?"

Barth is of the opinion that the foundation of the German Federal Republic and the concentration of military forces in Europe could hardly be considered by Russia as anything else but a provocation. The whole absurd armament race, moreover, was backed in the West by the theologians who canonized the collective man of the East as an angel of darkness and the organization man of the West as an angel of light. The Christian Churches according to Barth have identified themselves too cheaply "with the ill-conceived and poorly executed Western cause". Instead of this it would have been better if they had sounded a mature testimony about the fundamental nature of peace and about the expectation of the kingdom of God. By the way in which the Churches have now tackled the matter—"Rome in this respect was no better than Geneva and Geneva no better than Rome" —they have caused great damage to the cause of the Gospel: "Instead of opposing practical arguments against the atheism of the East, they have supplied it with new arguments that are harder to refute."

On the basis of these and similar thoughts, Barth has been very violently attacked, especially in Switzerland, "where there are a remarkably great number of little McCarthys".

In connection with the Hungarian crisis a comparison was made between Sartre and Karl Barth, which resulted in Barth's disadvantage: the penitent sinner against the hardened one who has fixed his teeth "in a grudge against America that is as incomprehensible as it is unchristian". Barth concluded his musings on this theme with some questioning sighs: "What would happen when the unholy Dulles-Adenauer era would one day come to an end? When the German Lutherans would retrace their evil tracks? When from the Vatican or from Geneva one day, no longer vague generalities but a prophetic apostolic word of peace and justice would sound forth? One hardly has courage left to hope for all this. But why should it be impossible that something like that would happen even before the end and the new beginning of all things?"

5

Christ in
the Center

The Basel period had been without a doubt the most fertile period in the whole of Karl Barth's active life. Besides the next ten volumes of the *Kirchliche Dogmatik* that were published from 1938, he also gave countless guest-lectures at home and abroad and published a lot of other important works.

In these years also took place Barth's second and third visit to the Netherlands. Already in 1926 he had visited Amsterdam where he gave a lecture at the Missionary Congress. His lecture on "Church and Culture" had caused quite a stir at the time in the phlegmatic ranks of its members who were as yet little accustomed to Barth's sonorous eschatological sounds. The Church, he stated, is the community of sinful men, called to life by God Himself, and who live by faith and by obedience to His Word. Culture then, is the task that is given to man but that man can never bring about because he is a sinner. Nevertheless, stumbling again and again, he must still try to complete this given task. "The recollection of the fact that God is in heaven and man on earth must not be an excuse for us to wrap up the talent we received and bury it." In every cultural activity man, however, must remember that true culture has only been given us as a promise of something that still is to be expected. "A general canonization of culture", Barth said, "such as Schleiermacher has rendered in the highest degree cannot be considered by us." Culture is, however, not only a promise for man but also a law of behavior. That this law is also capable of being fulfilled here on earth does not necessarily follow. The law demands obedience, but as sinners we cannot produce this obedience.

The end is unattainable: "It is not up to us to build the kingdom of God, there is no humanity in this world." Only with the Second Coming of Christ is a real, successful culture possibile. If we believe that we can anticipate this, we will fall, of necessity, not only into useless illusions but also into disobedience and rebelliousness. Exactly by keeping alive this hope for the gift of final consummation the Church remains true to herself and performs the best service to society.

One of Barth's listeners at Amsterdam wrote in the *Theologische Blätter* (Number 7) of 1926 a report on his lecture. In later years Barth would point to this report as an example of "the terrible inability to listen,

with which even the modern believer of good will
usually hears us".

But on the other hand, the Reverend Buskes can tell
us that not all of Barth's listeners in 1926 were
"modern listeners of good will".* He recounts what
a Reformed politician in those days wrote: "It is
remarkable that people are calling a Barth to come
here in order to learn from him how little progress
one makes with him, instead of telling him: Rather
come here to sit down as a pupil at the feet of the
Reformed theologians, in order to learn the first principles of the Reformed faith. . . . When a man like
Barth would come and stand before the Synod of
Assen in order to say: 'I have a message for you,'
then I think that he would get the answer: 'That may
be so, but we first have a message for you, because
we want to bow down in obedience to the certainty
of the Scriptures'."

Reverend Buskes can also further tell us as any
eye-witness of this first visit by Barth to the Netherlands that the overloaded program did not please Barth
at all. They wanted to carry him everywhere, show
him everywhere. But Barth sighed: "I would like so
much to go to a movie." At last they dropped the
rest of the program and visited Tuschinski theater,
the Ryksmuseum and Zandvoort beach. Neither did
Barth's following visits to the Netherlands always come
off without major or minor incidents. In 1935 and
1939 he made a tour of the theological faculties of
Groningen, Kampen, Utrecht, Amsterdam and Ley-
den. At Amsterdam the police objected to Barth's
lecture because he was going to answer questions

* J. J. Buskes, *Hoera voor het leven* (Amsterdam, 1959),
83-84.

about the Christian politics of Groen van Prinsterer and Abraham Kuyper, in which connection also the salaries of Protestant ministers would be discussed. It was feared that this would lead to a discussion of politics in general. In order to prevent embarrassing intervention by the police the meeting moved into another hall where a closed session was held. These and other things even led to questions in the Lower House of Parliament by the Social Democratic Labor Party.

These political side-phenomena probably did not enlighten Barth's vision on Dutch matters. Not only the action of the Amsterdam police made history. Barth's categorical dismissal of infant baptism as he clearly expressed it at Utrecht also especially brought Dutch sentiments to a boiling point. According to him, it would not be right that a recipient of baptism should be a passive object. According to Scripture, the baptismal candidate must be active, because he must receive baptism as the answer to a question really asked by himself. In the New Testament people are not brought in for baptism; they themselves come to be baptized. There is no place in Scriptures for those who have nothing to ask and to whom there is therefore nothing to answer. "I could only point to one thin thread", Barth said, "to which one might hold on for dear life to justify infant baptism in the New Testament. I am referring to the fact that in Act 16, 15; 18, 8, and 1 Corinthians 1, 16, there is mention of the baptism of a whole 'house' and Acts 16, 33, speaks of the baptism of the prison warden 'with all his family', in which case these expressions only make it not impossible to suppose that there were also children under age among them. However, one should also still pay attention in these places to the ever recurring order of things: preaching of the Word —faith—baptism, and then one may decide whether or not one should really hold on to this thin thread." Barth rejected the appeal to the faith of the Church, the parents or the godfather and godmother. According to him, there is no such thing as a vicarious faith, unless the faith of Christ. Luther and Calvin had also failed in this matter in Barth's opinion. The confusion into which both of them and their successors got themselves is really hopeless. "Within the great system of the doctrine on baptism, infant baptism can hardly be saved without exegetic and other tricks and sophisms—any proof against this has never yet been produced!"

Barth said he supposed that infant baptism was being maintained within Reformed circles for reasons that were theologically irrelevant. People did not want to give up infant baptism, he suggested, because they did not want to put the existence of the Protestant Church within the Constantinian *corpus christianum* in the balance; as for the present time, they did not want to hazard the current image of national Churches. "The [Dutch Reformed] Church in any case could no longer be the national Church and Established Church in the sense of the Church for the masses, when it would break with the practice of infant baptism. *Hinc, hinc illae lacrimae!*" (hence all those tears!)

That these and other theses of Barth caused the necessary commotion is completely understandable. Meanwhile, it is equally understandable that through the many problems that were laid before him in the Netherlands, mostly from considerations of a very different background, Barth has never very well understood or appreciated the complicated Church conditions in this country.

In spite of all those worries that his travels and journeys, meetings and debates entailed, Barth's greatest attention was more and more concentrated on the completion of his lifework, the *Kirchliche Dogmatik*. After 1935 one sees in his work a pronounced positive trend that, beside all his opposition to the "old" liberalism, will be of lasting significance. It has been said that in 1935 the period of his "consistent christology" began.

Neither philosophy, nor the history of religon, nor the historical method, but only the revealed Word that here and now confronts me is the basis of faith. This revealed Word is not an abstraction; it is the living Person of Christ Himself. The entire dogmatic science, the whole of theology must therefore continually be orientated christologically, and even all earthly realities ultimately cannot be properly defined except on the basis of our belief in Christ. Christ's Person and work constitute the only criterion of theology. Neither philosophy nor the traditions of the Church must ever take over this task. All this has far-reaching consequences. So, for example, the central theses about anthropology must be deducted from the humanity of Jesus Christ. It is, therefore, in Barth's opinion, wholly incorrect to interpret the christological dogma that the Council of Chalcedon defined, from a previously supposed anthropology. Chalcedon's definition that Jesus Christ is truly God and truly man is the formulation of a biblical datum that is an absolute starting point. Only from there can we understand "the" man as he can really be understood. Barth said very categorically: "Because the man Jesus is the revealing Word of God, He is therefore the fount of our knowledge about the human being created by God." The most important essential qualities of man—his being fellowman, his being composed of body and soul, his temporariness— can only be understood in their deepest reality on the basis of our belief in the God-man Jesus Christ. In the same way, only man's relationship with the Church founded by Christ can make us understand the real nature of the relationship that exists between man and woman and of the fertility of this interhuman alliance.

A central and extremely interesting part of Barth's theology was concerned with the doctrine of predestination. Here also he proceeded along new and, for many, totally unexpected paths, because his whole reflection was determined by his christological vision. Barth broke radically and in complete awareness with all previous Reformation concepts. It cannot be true that in treating this difficult problem one should have to speak not only about a Book of Life but also about a column of death notices. When that happens, one can only too easily understand Milton's complaint when he sighs: "Even if I should go to Hell, such a God (as in the Calvinistic doctrine of predestination) can never have my respect" (KD, vol. II, 2, p.12). As all this penetrated Barth's conscience more sharply, he became more strongly convinced that here also he would have to begin thinking very consistently from the standpoint of the biblical testimony about Christ. Appealing to Augustine, especially Calvin and his followers had understood predestination in the sense of a decision existing from all eternity in God, by which men are divided into two categories: those who were destined for eternal happiness and those who would be lost. Barth could not find this idea in the New Testament.

For him, divine predestination is the same thing as God's covenant of grace. All men are under God's anger, but all men are equally under God's eternal mercy. Estranged from Christ, all are rejected, but united with Him they are accepted in grace. Predestination is an act of God's mercy. It must therefore not give occasion to convulsive fear, but only to Christian joy. It is here a matter of the climax of the Gospel as the Good News.

These were merely some introductory remarks of Barth's, which already give us an inkling that he was entering upon an entirely unexpected road. The christological method of attacking the problem appeared already in the order in which he dealt with the mystery of predestination: (1) the choice of Christ, (2) the choice of the community, (3) the choice of the individual.

Christ is both the God who chooses and predestines, and the man who is radically chosen and predestined. It is only from this revelation in the incarnation that theology can try to say something meaningful about the mystery of the election. It then appears from Scripture that Christ is the electing God: from all eternity He chooses to fulfill the will of the Father, to deliver Himself and to descend upon the earth in order to bring God's covenant into reality. At the same time, however, it appears from Scripture that Christ is the Chosen One. The man Jesus Christ has been elected by God as the firstborn of all creation in order to exist as another being beside God, but also at the same time personally united with Him. In this way the fact of Christ being elected becomes the highest imaginable form of grace: the fact that this creature is taken up into God's own divine being.

When one completely follows Barth's thesis about our election in Christ, the question arises of whether in election there is then no negative, frightening aspect at all. Barth answered that there certainly is such a thing as rejection; however, not in the sense that all men are now to be divided into two classes. On the contrary: God has chosen for Himself rejection; for man, election to happiness. Our rejection, our sin and our death, God has taken all this upon Himself in Christ, in order that we might inherit God's glory. In the central mystery that was accomplished on the cross, God has taken upon Himself all human misery, the hell of death that is the manifestation of sin, and He has taken this upon Himself once for all (KD, vol. II, 2, p. 179). Sin is implied in the event of the incarnation. It is only thanks to God's antecedent and superabundant grace—the incarnation—that sin can exist: had the free man Jesus Christ not existed, then there would have been neither creation nor sin, but then also God would no longer have been Himself, namely, overflowing grace and mercy.

Since Barth's whole theological concept of man stands so consistently in the light of the revelation of Christ, it will also cause no surprise that his concept of sin is equally christologically founded. Only from the totality of what happened on Golgotha can it become clear what sin—or rather, sinful man—really is. Man as sinner appears to be atheist, fratricide and attacker of himself (KD, vol. IV, 1, p.441).

By his assault on Jesus Christ, the incarnate Son of God, the sinner appears to be the one who attempts an absurd assault on God. Because Christ is our fellow-man in whose image God has created every man, and in whom every man is honored or attacked, His murder is at the same time the unmistakable sign that sin is also fratricide. Finally, sin also attacks and destroys sinful man himself, because Christ is the eternal Word of God, by whom all things have been created. By attacking this creative Word, one saws off the branch on which one is sitting. The history of Judas who hanged himself after the betrayal illustrates this.

Also the classical question of the moralists, who still often practice their status as theologians in a remarkable way by speaking more about "nature" than about Christ, naturally comes under discussion here: What is it really that constitutes the wickedness of sin? Barth corrects the question: Who is really competent to qualify the human act in certain circumstances as "forbidden" or even "bad"? He then enumerates some possibilites taken from history: The voice of the individual conscience? The voice of the eternal law in the common human consciousness? The voice of certain norms that have been handed down by all peoples of all times to one another? Here also, however, it must ultimately be said that Jesus Christ is the only judge. He is the one "whose fan is in his hand; and he will thoroughly cleanse his floor and gather his wheat into the barn. But the chaff he will burn with unquenchable fire" (Matt. 3, 12). Christ alone can speak these words, because he pronounces them from a point where all men come from. He is the God-man, in whom God's law incarnates itself into a judicial personality present on earth. Human nature, which we carry in ourselves, has been created by God, based upon Christ who is our head.

In the life and death of Christ also, all human subtle attempts to escape from the seriousness of sin are unmasked. Too often one still looks upon sin as an external act, something accidental that does not really touch the inner personality, the substantial being of man. Because *the* man Christ has been made unto sin for us, it has thus been clearly demonstrated that evey man in his totality and all men without exception are sinful. It is true indeed that the sinner precisely moves away from the nature given to him by God, which is therefore good, and that he thus estranges himself from himself. But this can only be said in view of God in Christ, because it is only God's unchangeable fidelity to Himself that guarantees that man estranged from himself is not instantly destroyed. Only God's grace saves man from his absurd attempt at self-destruction (KD, vol. IV, 1, p.447).

It has gradually become the fashion to speak somewhat contemptuously about theological reflections that would not be out of place in a handbook of philosophy and logic. There are worse fashions than that. If, however, this sort of contempt does not go beyond a sterile declaration of discontent, it is not much help to theology.

As no one else before him, Barth has shown that a consistent approach to the whole theology from the central point of the Christ mystery is definitely possible. Because he has done real pioneer work and in spite of himself, still, on several points, uses and idealistically biased philosophy, his work will have to be revised on various points. More than anyone else, Barth himself is convinced of this. Perhaps nobody is more frightened of "Barthians" than Barth himself. Explicitly he wrote on this point: "I am really the last man who would not know that what has been offered here can be no more than the beginning of a new reflection on the Word of God. It is the beginning of a dialogue, necessary for the Church, with the doctrine of the last centuries, but also with that of the Reformation and with the old and the new Catholicism. Every dialogue with the older and younger pioneers can be conducted more profoundly than has been done here, just as every problem can be thought over more profoundly and more extensively in its context. But especially every line of Holy Scripture can, on the basis of newer explorations, become better understood and formulated than in my work. I do not look upon my work as a new *Summa Theologica,* which gives a sure support; on the contrary: many people will still be able to do very much and I would be glad to live to see the day when I would be thoroughly overtaken by someone or other, at least when it would be an overtaking on roads that really offer some perspective" (KD, vol. III, 4, vol. VIII).

In view of the incidents connected with Barth's succession, where a person was appointed whose theological tendencies were very clearly in the direction of Bultmann, there is something tragic in it when one hears Barth add these words, written in 1951: "One of the roads, however, that I do not yet see offering much perspective is the one that attempts to lay the foundation of all theology and exegesis with the aid of existential philosophy. Existentialism can indeed be a useful instrument—although certainly not the only or definitive one—and therefore it is understandable that especially the best among the students seize it with a kind of sensuality and make a rather passionate use of it. Until now, however, I cannot see that, where one has given oneself over to it, any worthwhile building has been done. For that matter I really do not see how it would be possible."

For the time being it is useful, not least of all for Catholic theologians, to make a careful study of Barth's consistent christocentric approach and where possible to adapt it to one's own theology. Perhaps it will then also appear that there is less need for "corrections" than one might originally have supposed.

The *Kirchliche Dogmatik* is not yet completed. Still to appear is the fourth volume of the fourth part, in which the consequences of the doctrine of the redemption for human actions will be discussed. According to an announcement in the Preface to Volume IV, 2, much attention will also be given in it to baptism and the last supper. After that, Barth has promised still a fifth part that will have eschatology as its subject. In spite of rumors from Basel that, after the ruling on the question of his successor, Barth said he had abandoned his plan for the final conclusion of his *Dogmatik,* we still hope that the man who once wrote that he lived like the followers of Nehemiah, the sword in one hand, the pen in the other, will be able to complete his lifework.

6

Barth's Importance
for Ecumenism

The hope that Barth will be able and willing to complete his lifework is not without self-interest. One may hope for it primarily in behalf of his fellow Protestants. His theology undoubtedly represents an enormous step forward compared to that of liberalism. Although his *Dogmatik* certainly did not meet with unqualified approval everywhere, and initial expectations were sometimes disappointed with the publication of a new volume, still no Protestant theologian henceforth will be able to ignore this work entirely except at his own cost.

For the sake of Catholic theology, one can only hope

73

that Barth will bring his work to a happy conclusion. The *Kirchliche Dogmatik* will prove of importance for the further development of the ecumenical dialogue. One who has heard Barth at the time of the first general meeting of the World Council of Churches in the Concertgebouw building at Amsterdam will hesitate to call him an ecumenical theologian. In our Introduction we have already made mention of the less flattering remarks that Barth permitted himself there with regard to Catholicism. To the well-known French Jesuit Daniélou, who asked him for clarification on this point, Barth again wrote clearly: "At Amsterdam not one of the many Churches approached the other with the pretense of being the only saving and infallible Church. This means that no one thought that by his very existence he had already answered the question that kept us all jointly occupied. This basis of our being together and working together would only have been broken by the presence of representatives of your Church. They could have taken their seats, not side by side with us, but only (visibly or invisibly) somewhere high on a throne above us. After all, among the poor there is no particular place for the rich, or among the hungry for the well fed, among the travelers for the one who has just comfortably settled down at his destination." The very fact that precisely Rome and Moscow did not come to Amsterdam suggested, according to Barth, that things were on the right path.

Whoever reads the often very eloquent polemics with Catholic theology in Barth's various works will still be confirmed in the impression that his Amsterdam words have left. Still one can continue with much justification to defend Barth's work as an important ecumenical contribution. Just as there is no such thing as a special kerygmatic theology that would be directly and exclusively meant for general consumption, there is also no place for such a thing as a special ecumenical theology. Where this is still attempted, one collaborates toward a further emptying out of theology. The building up of a separate kerygmatic theology, which would be aimed exclusively at the practice of evangelization and lives on the needs that exist there, proceeds from the fatal supposition that there would also exist a theology that would be unimportant for the practice of the life of the faith.

Although sometimes the traditional theological treatises indeed foster this supposition, one must not let oneself be tempted by the specimens of a bad kind of theology to a general verdict on all "systematic" theology. The only legitimate conclusion to which this phenomenon should lead is that the whole of theology must be brought in closer contact with the concrete experience of the life of the believing man. A more intensive participation of our Catholic laymen in theology is certainly needed for this, because the isolated position of the clergy must of necessity have its repercussion on the practice of theology, which so far has been mainly a clerical occupation.

If we want to get out of this deadlock by seeking refuge in a few artificially planted oases in the midst of the theological desert, this is a mere ostrich policy. Similarly, the whole of theology must be of such a nature that it lends itself to ecumenical contact. When one does not consider this as an integrally theological task, but only does a little raking up of one's theological front garden in order to be able to play host to some guests of a different creed, the disillusionment will be all the greater afterward. Not every guest is just a casual visitor. There will always be those—and often they are the best—who want to stay a little longer and would like to see the whole house. But should they then notice the old contra-reformatory designs in our wallpapaer, not to speak of the collection of nominalistic antiques that is still continually displayed—even if in some obscure corner—we have no right to be surprised if they no longer take our front garden very seriously. It is sometimes a little painful and sobering for well-intentioned, ecumenically minded theologians, when Protestant partners in the dialogue after an exchange of opinions finally still point again to the Catholic practices of piety and popular devotions. Even if this pointing is indeed not an airtight alibi, still such an appeal is sometimes quite *ad rem*. As long as receptivity to the theological contribution of others has not penetrated the daily life of the faith, there can be no question of any large-scale ecumenical rapprochement.

When theology really inclines itself to the mystery of God's revelation and in so doing invites co-thinking and co-meditating in the whole of the area of the faith, then it is both kerygmatic and ecumenical. He puts things sometimes very pointedly, and he does this consciously, because in the long run cheap, superficial agreements do not help us very much. He does this sometimes also in an agressive and irritable tone. But one who knows him more intimately will remember here also that barking dogs rarely bite. Barth is an extremely temperamental person, and moreover a great stylist of the German, *i.e.,* rather long-winded in expresing himself. Where these qualities meet, one may expect that an initially sober dismissal of a thesis or a person may sometimes, in the course of writing, expand into a violent or somewhat heated polemic. Besides, there is every chance that Barth himself in a Preface to a following publication will reduce this again to its right proportions. In the third volume of his *Dogmatik* the Dutch *"neo-Calvinists"* received a thorough working over because they had called Barth a monist and even had the nerve *sich mit unwiederholbaren Worten an W. A. Mozart zu vergreifen* (to unjustly attack W. A. Mozart with words that bear no repetition). Four years later it seemed that Berkouwer's book *De triomf der genade in de theologie van Karl Barth* (The Triumph of Grace in Karl Barth's Theology) had put him in a somewhat milder mood. Then he wrote: "Man's anger rarely does what is good in God's eyes, and surely not when he makes an outburst *in globo*."

The one who confuses ecumenical theology with a somewhat vague pietism or with a worn-down fundamentalism comes to the wrong man in Barth. The fact, however, that in the deeply theological sense of the word he greatly enhances the ecumenical discussion appears among other things also from the number of important works in the Catholic camp that occupy themselves with him. Barth gave them every reason for this. Repeatedly he expressed his opinion on Catholicism. We have already quoted his famous statements about the analogy of being in the Preface to *Kirchliche Dogmatik* (vol. I, 1). On March 9, 1928, Barth gave a lecture in Bremen entitled "Roman Catholicism as a Question to the Protestant Church." Later he gave this lecture again at Osnabrück and Düsseldorf. There he began with the gen-

eral statement that in the dialogue every man seems
to be more concerned with saying something himself
and convincing the other as his opponent, rather than
in occupying himself seriously with the questions of
his partner in the dialogue. Always one feels in himself
the little Socrates, who seeks by shrewd questions to
convert the other to his own truth. According to Barth
the Protestant Church also often feels itself thus
restricted in the dialogue with Catholics. Against this
attitude Barth made a stronge plea at Bremen that
just for once one should also listen quietly to the
questions that Catholics want to put, and he advised
his fellow Protestants not to act as if they were in
possession of the ready-made truth. Nor did Barth
let himself be prevented in this by the conviction he
still expressed on that occasion, that neither Przywara
nor Karl Adam, Hogu Lang nor Romano Guardini
would ever feel called upon to do the same thing on
their part. Even the prospect that, in the lower
regions of inter-confessional polemics—as he put it—
one will play off his lecture as an argument for Catholicism is no reason to bypass the real questions of
Catholicism.

There are especially two questions that Barth sees
Catholicism put to the Churches of the Reformation:
(1) to what extent, if any, is Protestanism really a
Church? (2) and to what extent, if any, is Protest-
anitsm a *Protestant* Church? With regard to the former
question: the Reformation did not want a destruction
of the Church but a restoration. The goal of this
restoration ought to be that the Church would become
more a house of God and less a house of men. Liberal
Protestantism, however, according to Barth, had
obscured all this in the worst possible manner. He

did not hesitate to add: "If on this very day I would become convinced that the interpretation given to the Reformation by the neo-liberal school of Schleiermacher—Ritschl—Toreltsch (or even Seeberg and Holl) was the correct one, in other words that Luther and Calvin really meant it like that, then indeed I would not become a Catholic tomorrow, but I would take my leave of the so-called Evangelical Church and, faced with a choice between the two, I would surely even rather become a Catholic." Barth thought in 1928 that his fellow Protestants ought to ask themselves in all sincerity whether they actually still knew what *Church* really is. The very fact that the Reformers opposed the meriting of grace and an unbloody renewal of the sacrifice of the cross showed that they really wanted to make the house of the Church again the house of God, Barth thinks. Protestant Church life, profoundly influenced by Schleiermacher, must permit Rome also to ask the question concerning to what extent it is Protestant. Almost nothing has remained of the renewal that the Reformation brought about as a protest. The Reformers wanted to restore the Church again as the instrument of God's Word, but the liberals and the pietists had relapsed into the cult of a static and attainable "supernature". This pietistic movement within Protestantism has made us forget the seriousness of our sinfulness, Barth says. Specifically the fact that sin affects our whole human existence, and therefore cannot be forgiven by any meritorious work on our part but exclusively by God's grace, had also fallen into oblivion again in Protestantism.

Catholicism *was* a question for Barth and not merely

an academic problem. The violence with which from
time to time he opposed it was, among other things,
also caused by the menacing proximity of this problem.
As a consequence of Barth's protesting the overemphasis on experience of pietistic Protestantism and
his bold clarion-call for a return to biblical objecti-
vism, it seemed to many that he was tending toward
Catholicism. Instead of focusing on man as led by
the Spirit, Barth again placed God and Christ in the
center of things. Between the publication of the
revised *Römerbrief* and Barth's lecture (discussed
previously) in Bremen, the transition of Erik Peterson
to the Catholic Church had already taken place. In
the early years he had been a zealous columnist for
Barth's magazine, in which he wrote about the function of theology and about matters of interest in
Church History. When this promising personality,
along with Oskar Bauhofer, went over to Catholicism,
there was of course every reason to sound the alarm.
So after all! Barth really *did* drive his people in the
direction of Rome.

Against the background of these sometimes very
violent reproaches from his fellow Protestants, it is
perfectly understandable that, wherever possible,
Barth, made a stand against Catholicism. He still
continues to carry on polemical discussions with Peterson, with much understanding and without personal
rancor. On our side when it is possible without
blushing to appeal to Schleiermacher, then one can
equally appeal to Thomas Aquinas. Both are equally
far removed from Luther and Calvin, he told Peterson.
Since then the two theologians have had little contact
with each other. Peterson soon left for Rome as professor at the Pontifical Institute of Christian Archae-

logy, where he wrote many learned articles, as dry as
stale loaves of rye bread, but every time with some
entirely unexpected point. That the fire of the Spirit
kept burning in this able patrologist he proved with
such brilliant little contributions as "Over het lachen
van Sara" (About Sarah's Laughing) and his sublime
articles in the French magazine *Dieu vivant*. On one
more occasion Barth and Peterson crossed swords and
notably about a subject over which few theologians
can still get excited: the doctrine on the angels. With
his nearly inexhausitble knowledge of the ancient
Christian traditions, Peterson had written a book in
which he extensively illustrated the liturgical function
of the angels. In the surprisingly extensive section that
Barth devotes to the angels in his *Dogmatik,* he
rejected certain parts of Peterson's view. Angels are
authorized messengers of God on earth. To accept
the existence of angels who would be wholly dedicated
to the divine liturgy without acting in the service of
God on earth, as Peterson accepted, was impossible
for Barth.

During the same years Barth also carried on a
controversy with Erich Przywara about the concept
of the Church. In the background, however, there
hovered especially the problem of the analogy, of
which Przywara had shown himself a fervent defender,
while, on the contrary, Barth thought that he could
clearly demonstrate the catastrophical consequences
of this doctrine of analogy in ecclesiology.

As the years went by the dialogue grew. On various
occasions Barth would complain that his theological
development was followed with more interest by
Catholics than by Protestants. Especially the works
of Hans Urs von Balthasar, Henri Bouillard and Hans
Küng have made an agreeable impression on him.

Von Balthasar is a fellow citizen of Barth's and is looked upon by him as a good friend. On top of the Bruderholz where Barth lives—called Mount Horeb by the students—extensive theological discussions developed in which Barth felt himself better understood than in many Protestant renderings of his work. Somewhere he remarked in passing that the development of his way of thinking from the rather negative period of the *Römerbrief* to his consistent christology "has been incomparably much better understood" by von Balthasar than "in the small library that has gradually mounted up around me." Von Balthasar did not surrender himself to Barth uncritically. Even apart from the contents of Barth's doctrine he admired the latter's style as much as his great systematic genius. But there remained penetrating questions that were programmatic for the future of the ecumenical dialogue. One is mentioned by von Balthasar: Can the distinction that Barth makes between the analogy of being and what one might call the analogy of faith really be maintained? And then above all: Is not the whole of Barth's theology after all—in spite of himself —too strongly influenced by a Hegel-inspired philosophy?

Also Henri Bouillard's three-volume work gives testimony of a great appreciation of Barth's theology, but all the same does not face him without reserve. This study had been offered as a dissertation to the Faculty of Arts and Philosophy of the Sorbonne. In the examination committee such well-known persons as Henri Gouhier and Jean Wahl had taken their places on the board. Barth was present at the public defense on May 16, 1956, in Paris. However, he could not take part in the discussions, which for a great part concerned the interpretation of his doctrine, something that caused some strange situations. The strict academic protocol of the Sorbonne made no provision for the possibility that a dissertation would ever be accepted about an author who was still living. It is not surprising that Bouillard, who already in the turbulent times of the *nouvelle theologie* wrote about the relation between nature and supernature, also used this problem as a frame of reference for his reflections on Barth. In spite of much that he admired as good in Barth he still reproached him for not entirely correctly interpreting the doctrine of Paul, by which Barth would also minimize the value of "good works". Texts in which Paul turns against the works of the law were brought up by Barth as arguments against the works of faith. Bouillard was also of the opinion—against Küng—that in Barth's view on justification, human existence was not really in its deepest essence sanctified by God. Maybe he would have judged a little more mildly on this point after taking cognizance of the following parts of the *Kirchliche Dogmatik*.

Bouillard recognized the great merits of Barth in the matter of the doctrine of predestination, although he noticed a danger that indeed was not imaginary. Because the possibility could not at all be excluded that if one would continue reasoning according to Barth's principles, one would have to arrive at the acceptance of a kind of total cosmic reconciliation. This theory, according to which ultimately no one can be definitely and for all eternity lost, has been highlighted in antiquity especially by Origen. Although this appeared on the horizon of Barth's doctrine in his christological interpretation of pre-

destination, he still tried to avert it by his concept of
the act of faith. The election is announced to us in the
preaching of revelation. This election therefore
becomes effective precisely in the responsive attitude
of the faith. Whoever does not believingly consent
to be in Christ is also at that very moment not in Him.
The very measure in which a man responds believingly
or unbelievingly to the message of revelation will
determine whether the old condemnation will again
descend on this man, or else eternal blessing. Whether
the man, to whom the word of election is addressed,
merely affirms that in spite of this he still will lead the
life of one rejected or really the life of one elected
is not decided by the promise itself. This decision takes
place exclusively in the existential surrender of faith.
Bouillard pointed out correctly that this solution of
Barth's, in which he attempted to avoid an Origen-
like doctrine of *apokatastasis,* was crossed by another
consideration, according to which faith only manifests what has already been given objectively. In that
consideration, which Barth also often used, faith is
the subjective recognition of what has already once
for all taken place in Christ, independently of man's
knowledge and action. That which is, becomes revealed in faith.

Bouillard's work was ecumenically of such great
importance because in all serenity a clear insight into
Barth's basic vision was given for the benefit of the
French-speaking public. Particularly because of
Barth's more German-oriented style of writing and
thinking, Bouillard had necessary difficulties with him.
He warned explicitly: "The French reader, who is
accustomed to a more compact *exposé,* to a more
analytical and more direct composition, will become

especially discouraged (*déconcerté*) here." The fact that in spite of this initial discouragement he has opened up such a great part of Barth's thinking to the Catholic French-speaking public augurs well for the ecumenical dialogue. Also the confrontation and mutual fecundity of the heterogeneous French and German styles of thinking may contribute to the ecumenical dialogue becoming more general, *i.e.*, more "catholic" in a Europe that is painfully searching for unity.

With a certain anxiety Barth waited for the reactions to the book of the young Swiss theologian Hans Küng, which caused a big stir on its publication in 1957. The author, who had studied at Rome's German College, meanwhile also became well known through his broad-minded publications regarding the Council. For several years now he has been teaching at Tübingen as successor of Heinrich Fries, also well known in ecumenical circles. In his doctral dissertation for the Institut Catholique of Paris, *Rechtfertigung, Die Lehre Karl Barths und eine katholische Besinnung* (Justification: The Teachings of Karl Barth and a Catholic Reflection), Küng defended a daring thesis. Investigating a central theme of Barth's theology, he felt justified to conclude that there is no essential difference between a correct interpretation of Barth's doctrine and the just as carefully interpreted decisions of the Council of Trent. In a Preface to this book Karl Barth himself has expressed his great surprise concerning this thesis, adding that at any rate Küng's interpretation of *his* (Barth's) doctrine was correct. With a touch of irony he wrote about this: "When that which you derive from Holy Scripture, from the old

and new Roman Catholic theology and then also from
Denzinger and therefore also from the texts of the
Council of Trent, when all this is indeed the doctrine
of your Church and can be confirmed as such, then
I will after all have to hurry a third time to the Santa
Maria Maggiore at Trent, where I have been twice
before to have a dialogue with the *genius loci*. This
time, however, in order to make a contrite confession:
Patres peccavi! . . ." (Fathers, I have sinned!)

The reactions for which Barth was waiting have
come. Probably after all they have given him a better
insight into the manifold business of Catholic theology
than he had before. Until then, he often gave the
impression that in order to get to know the opinion
of "the" Catholic theology a simple consulting of
Denzinger was enough. By now it must have become
clear to him — by physical association — that even
among Catholic theologians there are birds of a very
great variety of feathers. And even among those who
wear the same religious habit there are still very great
differences possible. Well-known figures such as Professor Groot in the Netherlands, Philips and Malevez
in Belgium, Fries, Stakemeier and Ratzinger in Germany came to the conclusion that not only had
Küng correctly interpreted Barth—that was something Barth himself had already made known—but
also that his interpretation of Trent was correct and
orthodox.

Almost every self-respecting commentator feels
himself called upon to introduce small corrections, or to point to something else that ought to
have been said, or said better. But the enumerated
authors assured Barth very positively that in Küng's
book he did not encounter a caricature of the Catholic

doctrine of justification, but a serious and generally convincing representation. There were others whose judgment was much more negative. The most important of these condemnatory critics were Ebneter in Germany and especially Stirnimann in Switzerland. As was expected, part of the critics kept to the middle road: moderate optimism or, as one wrote: admittedly a fundamental aggreement has been demonstrated, but not a total one. This formulation originated from the Spanish critic Alfaro, in whom Barth could also learn that understanding for his teaching also among the Spanish theologians went deeper than one probably expected. The Spanish-language area had indeed already been able to get acquainted with Barth very early through the work of Ortega y Gasset, but especially of Unamuno, who had found his track via Kierkegaard.

Küng defended that Barth's view of the central position of Christ also with regard to creation must necessarily be accepted. It is the teaching of Scripture. All things have been created in Christ, so that a separation between nature and supernature must not be held as the necessary inventory of Catholic theology. Creation and the history of salvation are right from the start aimed at one another and intimately connected. Also the good that remains in the sinner is not a little piece of uncorrupted nature that continues to exist outside Christ. When man is not destroyed in his sin he owes this to Christ who has saved him for justification.

Küng further insisted firmly that also in Catholic theology justification must first be seen as a *declaration* of justification that takes place in God. When one reflects—Küng says—that what Barth and many other

Protestant theologians understand by justification is often rendered by Catholics in the word "redemption", then this becomes much clearer. The notion "objective redemption" has already long since become current in Catholic theology. "If Barth had been conscious of this, his criticism of the Council of Trent would have been different." On the other hand, Küng pointed out that in Barth's view justification does not really remain "forensic": in God's *declaration* of justification something real also happens *in man himself*. God's Word does not return from the earth empty-handed. Our being children of God and heirs to heaven mean a reality in the one justified. With Romans 8, 17 and 1 Peter 1, 3, Barth maintained unequivocally that we are God's children, born anew unto a living hope. If in the writing of his dissertation Küng could already have referred to the second part of the fourth volume of Barth's *Dogmatik,* he might have quoted from it to confirm this interpretation of Barth's teaching with even greater power of persuasion.

In his Preface to Küng's book Barth said that he hailed this work—just like Noah from the window of his ark—as a clear sign that the flood of the times in which Catholic and Protestant theologians either were facing one another only polemically, or were willing to speak to each other in some noncommittal pacificism, but mostly not at all, is indeed not yet past, but is at least slowly receding. He expressed the hope that no one among Küng's readers will be so foolish as to call Barth a crypto-Catholic or Küng a crypto-Protestant. As a guiding principle for a continued ecumenical development, Barth propagates: proceeding from what unites us, discuss what separates us in view of what unites us. In these words and in Barth's entire later work one hears unmistakably an authentic ecumenical awareness. The tone or his dissertations on Catholicism has become more matter-of-fact, and above all, he has learned to understand that what the Catholic handbooks offer as theology is by far not always covered by today's theological way of thinking. It has also become clearer to him that the pronouncements of the teaching authority of the Church must be interpreted carefully and with deliberation. The definitions of the Council of Trent had been formulated against a very specific historical background and just as no historical document must be discussed apart from its historical context, neither should Trent. This is all the more urgent because the Fathers of the Council of Trent were standing exactly in a conscious antithesis to the Reformation. Some formulations and accentuations from the 16th-century Catholic theology can only be rightly understood if one takes proper account of this oppositional attitude.

Apparently it is not always easy for our Protestant partners in the dialogue to appreciate this sufficiently. It is one of the most painful experiences of the ecumenical dialogue when one realizes that at a given moment good faith is held in doubt. This happens not infrequently at the moment when a greater agreement in doctrine is established than one ever expected before. It still always happens that one reproachfully points out to us some official ecclesiastical documents or airtight formulations from some timeless handbook in which it says "different". With a certain mistrust it then may be suggested that the Catholic partner in the dialogue is not completely

honest. He would have fashioned the clear doctrine
of his Church a little according to the need of the
moment in order to make a good score with it. But
Rome really has a different opinion on it, they think.
This view obviously proceeds from the incorrect
supposition that Catholic thought on the faith is a
monolithic block, petrified for all eternity into a
massive rockland that, once it has been mapped by
Denzinger or if need be by a Diekamp, has now by
papal decree been declared for all eternity a recrea-
tional ground in which one can never lose his way.
Eruptions and landslides seem to be excluded here.
The signposts for theological tourists have been placed
with deliberation on all doubtful junctions at the same
time by a central organization; it is possible to make
walking-trips of an hour or of a whole day, but in
principle there is nothing new to discover. Insofar as
the foundation of the faith has been given once and
for all in Christ and the Church, they are right.
Insofar as Christianity and the reflection on the data
of faith are essentially incarnatory, they are wrong.
Even Catholics themselves might be more deeply convinced of this truth. Insofar as they do not sufficiently realize this, the Catholic theologian must not
blame his Protestant partner too much if he is too
little conscious of it as yet.

    In view of all this it was of great ecumenical signifi-
cance that also Karl Rahner, one of today's most
important Catholic theologians, unequivocally took
Küng's side. His completely positive attitude to the
latter's work can hardly be too much appreciated.
Without any reservation Rahner declared to Barth:
"Küng's rendering of the doctrine of justification is
Catholic." And when Barth declared, "If your render-

ing is correct, then there is no essential difference
between us on this point," Rahner added that such a
declaration really ought to be greeted with more
enthusiasm than was the case to his knowledge. Further in his extensive discussion, which has been
included in the fourth volume of his *Schriften zur
Theologie* (*Theological Investigations*), Rahner then
addressed himself especially to those Catholics who are
afraid that after all no fundamental agreement was
really reached. Any agreement between men about a
certain truth is never exactly verifiable. Every agreement, every compromise struggles with a laborious
formulation. Because our words are never a total and
adequate expression of our inner conviction, every
verbal agreement among men is always threatened,
precarious and fragile. But that is as far as we can get.
If one says as man that one recognizes oneself in what
the other man says, then there *is* agreement. Ultimately one can go on doubting everything, as long
as one cannot obtain an exactly verifiable, mathe-
matical certainty.

In every human encounter, however, this form of
certainty is excluded. Those who, in connection with
Küng's book, continue to ask themselves whether one
has now "really" and "profoundly" come to agreement on this point of justification, Rahner reproached
as maintaining a neurotic anxiety. No man can see
in the heart of his fellowman, only God can do this.
When in an honest dialogue one comes to a verbal
agreement, then the highest that is attainable among
men has been reached. The fact that one comes to the
same conclusion from a different starting point will
give a specific color to our expressions. Completely
identical wording is excluded here. But this same

phenomenon also appears within Catholic theology itself, when an orthodox Thomist and an orthodox Molinist voice their opinions on grace and human liberty. Küng's sensational book became the cause for different, not always equally mature speculations. A Spanish commentator who, in spite of Barth's own specific warning, gave his commentary the significant title *Karl Barth, un cripto católico? . . .*, felt it incumbent upon himself amid the reigning optimism to sound the warning that a complete agreement between Barth and Rome would really be quite a while in coming after all, certainly as long as there would remain such important points of disagreement on the concept of the Church.

The optimism, however, was no longer easy to check. A year later Küng's predecessor at Tübingen, Heinrich Fries, who had been called to Munich, published an article in *Catholica,* the German magazine for ecumenical theology, in which he critically investigated Barth's teachings on the Church. If the Spanish commentator has read Fries' article, then he must necessarily have come to the conclusion that now indeed all barriers between Barth and Rome have been lifted, Fries says nothing more or less than that Barth's ecclesiology "insofar as it has been published till now, does not justify any schism within the one Church".

Although it is difficult to follow entirely this far-reaching conclusion by Fries, it still remains a remarkable fact that a well-known theologian could arrive at such a conclusion. It is therefore desirable to scrutinize Fries' thesis further by taking a closer look at the development that Barth's ecclesiology has undergone. This development is in a certain sense symptomatic of the development of his entire theology, as presented above. Moreover, it also becomes clear that Barth still has never completely disavowed himself. Precisely this last fact is a reason for us not to adopt Fries' statement without qualification. The main line of Barth's thinking is more or less clear enough. Initially his theology had grown as a defense: it is "apologetic" in orgin. The current liberal theology sinned by what Barth has sometimes called *Schleiermacherei* ("Schleiermacherizing"). The infinite distinction between God and world was so much neglected that a reflection about the doctrine of faith was in danger of degenerating into a more or less pious experimental science. The possibility of proof by experience reigned supreme. The human subject had become starting point and central point to such a degree that the attention to the self-revelation of God had been pushed to second place. So against this imperceptible secularization of theology Barth came in rebellion. The great discovery of his first period was the infinitely qualitative difference between God and world, between eternity and time. This rediscovery led Barth to what his first critics have rather bluntly called a form of dualism. They compare the author of the programmatic conmmentary on the *Römerbrief* with Marcion, who denied the reality of Christ's earthly appearance, because according to him there exists an insurpassable abyss between the God of grace and the reality of this world. All this is also reflected in Barth's ecclesiology.

7

Barth's Teaching
on the Church

In Barth's first period his doctrine on the Church
was also clearly determined by a dualistic tendency.
The Church and world are of a piece and therefore
ultimately in radical opposition to God. Although
there exists a dialectical tension between Church and
world, this opposition disappears before the absolute
and all-overshadowing opposition between time and
eternity. Seen in this light, therefore, the distinction
between Church and world is no greater than the distinction that exists between nature and culture, mate-
rialism and idealism, capitalism and socialism, im-
perialism and democracy. In the light of eternity, all

these oppositions prove ultimately to be merely relative and of secondary importance because they are only distinctions within the world.

"In relation to the Gospel, the Church stands as the incarnation of the ultimate human possibility this side of the impossible possibility of God. Here yawns the abyss as nowhere else" (*Hierklafft der Abgrund wie nirgends sont*), we read in the *Römerbrief* (second edition, p. 316). The radical opposition between God and world finds even its most striking expression in the case of the Church. Because in the Church the things of the other world "have become another metaphysical reality and thus a mere extension of the things of this world".* Barth waxes especially eloquent here: the Church is the place where one knows and possesses all sorts of things about God, where God—from an unknown beginning and end—has been shifted in some way or other to the known middle, where one no longer needs to meditate about death in order to become wise, but where one immediately *possesses* faith, hope and charity, immediately *is* God's child, immediately *waits* for God's kingdom and *works* toward it—as if those were things that one could be and possess, that one would expect to work for. The Church, Barth said, is the more or less energetic attempt to humanize the divine, to temporalize it, to make it a thing. In the Church one attempts to secularize the transcendental, living God, to render comprehensible the incomprehensible but unavoidable road. After a sideways lunge at Catholicism, "where one can get better results in all these things", Barth

* Barth distinguishes between the *Jenseits*—that which is of the Other Side—and the *Diesseits*—that which is of This Side (Translator).

then came to the final conclusion: "The Gospel is the abolition of the Church, just as the Church is the abolition of the Gospel"—at which point he does not fail to refer to Dostoevski's grand inquisitor.

However paradoxical it may sound, still in all this there is also exactly the reason why man, according to Barth, must not withdraw himself from the Church. He must become conscious of our absolute sinfulness and darkness and this takes place in the earthly, visible Church. Exactly as an evangelical Christian, one has to take the Church seriously, even exteremely seriously, he said. To be a Church is something that is bound to fail, because in itself it is impossible of realization. But it is an impossibility that is inherent in man's being merely human, an impossibility that ultimately is due to the fact that we lack the magnificence of God. To accept this destiny, to throw in one's lot with humanity then means to become profoundly conscious within the Church of one's lack of God.

In expectation of the definitive breakthrough of God's transcendental grace, the Church community has to live by the promise. And in the measure in which one becomes more strongly conscious of his sinfulness and of the fragility of everything earthly, including the Church, he will be able to live more radically out of Christian hope. And this is ultimately what matters. "A Christianity that is not completely and without any reservation eschatology has completely and without any reservation nothing to do with Christ" (*Römerbrief*, second edition, p.300).

In the first period of Barth's ecclesiology the Church is standing plainly on the side of the promise, not of the fulfillment. She is only a very provisional reality. The visible Church must in no way labor under the

conception that within herself the divine transcendence
has appeared tangible and available on earth.

This thinking in terms of dialectical opposition,
inspired by the controversy over liberal theology, has
slowly given way in Barth to a more synthetic view.
One could represent the complete change that has
come about in Barth's manner of thought somewhat
systematically and therefore somewhat too strongly
by saying that in this respect he has also developed
from an initial dualism to a kind of christocentric
monism. This is connected with the previously mentioned central position that the doctrine of the incarnation has begun to take in Barth's theology. In Christ,
God's grace has become an earthly reality, in Him the
redeeming love of God has taken the appearance "of
a created objectivity" (KD, vol. II, 1, p.56). One
cannot deny that this view already sounds much more
familiar to the ears of Catholic theologians. The
definition that Barth gives here reminds us immediately of the concept of a "sacrament", because a sacrament is indeed an earthly reality, in which God's
invisible operation of grace assumes a visible form.
Barth himself therefore is now most assuredly going
so far as to bring Church and sacrament explicitly into
connection: "The Church on its objective side is sacramental, which means that she must be understood in
the analogy of baptism and the last supper" (KD,
vol. I, 2, p.253).

This concept of Barth's is connected with his
christocentrism. If one continues to look at the Church
mainly from the point of view of man, one must
necessarily come to such relativizing ideas as Barth
defended in his *Römerbrief*. There is, however, another idea that completes this. Just as the deepest

essence of man can only be disclosed through the man Jesus Christ, in the same way also the Church can only be fully comprehended through the Lord of the Church, Christ. This has some important consequences. Through Christ the Word of God has resounded in the world. This Word is supremely powerful and according to the Scriptures does not return void: it has been heard and it has created life on this barren earth. This life of those who have been accepted in Christ is the life of the Church. Therefore one can rightly say that outside the Church there is no salvation (KD, vol. I, 2, p. 235). Since the Church is thus continually being reborn from the life of Christ, she cannot even *want* to fall back to the stage of human self-justification. If the Church would still want to withdraw herself from this supreme power of grace, then she would stop being the Church. This is impossible, however, because grace remains itself, because the divine Word constantly effects salvation anew. At the same time, it becomes clear here that the Church is really a community. There is only one life, the being of the Word of God. "Those who are in the Church *are* indeed brothers and sisters" (KD, vol. I, 2, p. 237). When they express this fundamental situation, they are carrying out, they are realizing this "being-Church". That is why the disputed thesis "outside the Church no salvation" must be clarified further: by belonging to Christ, one belongs to all those who are in Christ. Outside this basic community man is lost.

Finally, Barth draws another important conclusion from the fact that the Church originates from Christ: she is also necessarily visible. Christ was in His human nature the historical revelation of God's redemptive will. God remains Himself in absolute transcendence: but with us. "If, however, He is God with us, then He is this historical reality, because we live and exist in historical reality. If this revelation of God in historical reality did not occur in vain, when there corresponds to the time He had for us, a time that we may have for Him, then the life of the children of God, the Church, is therefore also visible." Obviously, this does not exclude the invisible element in the Church. Just as it remained invisible in the incarnation that the very Word of God appeared in time, so also in the Church scandal and trials of the faith remain possible. But it still remains a fact that the children of God are visible men, who are brought together by a visible event of salvation. "That they have received God's revelation is invisible, but they themselves are visible as those who are obliged and willing to commemorate that revelation. That it concerns *God's* calling voice is invisible, but the event of their being called together is visible. That their unity, which is the Word of God they have heard, is invisible, but visible is the fact that they belong together and stay together" (KD, vol. I, 2, p.240). That is why Barth now also says that the thesis "outside the Church no salvation" also implies that for every man subjectively the reality of the revelation always and everywhere takes place in an historical meeting and decision, which are visible and can be imagined and experienced.

As soon as Barth began to express himself in this vein, the critics, who had followed him in his first (more "dualistic") period with difficulty but in the end wholeheartedly, thought that they ought to sound a warning. They wanted to exorcize the new Barth by means of the old one—something that since

then happened repeatedly. They already had visions
of the venerated master drifting off into the Roman
channel. Barth knew of this accusation and defended
himself by energetically opposing it. But he refused
to let himself be pushed in another direction by such
an attack. It is therefore not surprising that he can
now appreciate more positively the biblical expression
for the Church as the "Body of Christ". When Paul
describes the Church like that, Barth says, then surely
one of the meanings that must be attached to this
title is that the Church "while being totally different,
is still a repetition of the same kind ... of the incarnation of the Word of God in the Person of Jesus Christ"
(KD, vol. I, 2, p.235). He purposely chooses the
word "repetition" here. According to Barth one must
not speak of a continuation or extension of the incarnation, because then one would be detracting from the
unique position of the objective revelation in Christ.

In a consistent pursuit of Barth's incarnatory view
on the Church, one comes to conclusions that are not
far removed from Catholic ecclesiology. The question
is only whether Barth himself also explicitly accepts
responsibility for these conclusions, which in our
opinion are obvious. Only too often we apply in our
scientific discussions and dialogues a rather doubtful
procedure by attributing opinions to a partner in the
dialogue as conclusions that in our opinion he really
ought to draw, even if he persistently does not pro-
nounce them. Now it is more than clear that Barth
consciously persists in opposing Catholic ecclesiology.
Perhaps this is also caused partly by the signals of
alarm of his fellow Protestants who saw him drifting
off toward Rome. However this may be, it would be
incorrect and one-sided not to pay due attention to

Barth's explicit criticism. Therefore we must also dwell a moment on it.

The Church is a sign—just as the humanity of Christ—but ultimately this really means, Barth insists, that we are here dealing with an act of God. God remains the sovereignly free Lord and in His hand He moves the Church as an instrument, "Given this sign and this instrument, this still does not mean that the self-revealing God Himself now, as it were, has become a part of this world or that He now after all has fallen into the hands of men assembled into a Church, who could dispose of Him at will.... We here touch a point where the Protestant and the Catholic concept of the Church are sharply opposed to one another", Barth thinks (KD, vol. I, 2, pp.247-248).

The background of what Barth says here is probably this: according to Catholic ecclesiology the Church has somehow become an independent entity side by side with God. Because the instrument has been taken out of God's hand, man can now freely and arbitrarily make use of it. That which in God's hand was a real mystery, man can now penetrate from all sides; he himself can define the limits where the Church is still operative in its sanctifying work and those where she is not. Thus it has become impossible to *believe* in the Church. Also with regard to the authority of Holy Scripture, Barth argued against the Catholic concept of Church. According to him the exclusive authority of the Scriptures is being done injustice by the Church of Rome and to such an extent that he does not hesitate to call "the autonomy of the Church the explicit essence of Catholicism" (KD, I, 2, p.639).

Also in the following parts of his *Dogmatik* Barth

does not change his position in this regard. We have already seen that he is prepared indeed to defend the visibility of the Church. He even does this with fervor, because an ecclesiological docetism is also a heresy. This real visibility is, however, only a partial aspect of the totality. What the Church is in reality, only the faithful can perceive. Here again the Catholic thinks that he is hearing sounds in which he indeed recognizes himself. After all, it has been quite some time since the apologetic period when we thought that—with an appeal to the famous expression of Bellarmine, "The Church is as visible as the Venetian Republic"—we could by means of an airtight argumentation indentify all the essential qualities of the Church of Christ in the Church of Rome.

Recently, when an American office of investigation, after undoubtedly thorough research, came to the conclusion that the Catholic Church was one of the world's best-organized and best-directed enterprises, with an even higher rating than a worldwide enterprise such as the Shell Oil Company, perhaps the editors of some Catholic papers may have promoted this triumphantly to front-page news, but the theologians could not have cared less. This kind of visibility is of an entirely different order than the *sacramental* visibility of the Church, in which a third dimension, God's sanctifying activity in Christ, is shown under a veil.

That this sacramental vision of the Church has also in Catholicism again more clearly penetrated man's conscience apparently escapes Barth. In Pope Pius XII's encyclical *Mystici Corporis* he no longer sees any place to *believe* in the Church. The encyclical, according to Barth, does not, to be sure, go so far as to identify

the notions "Mystical Body" and "Church of Rome",
but one still finds in it an unequivocal equalizing of the
mystery of the Church, founded by Christ and continually kept alive by Him, and of her historical
activity and juridical organization. "What the Church
really is", Barth says in connection with the encyclical,
"that is in no way hidden, and has no need of being
believed, can be read immediately from what is visible
as Church, from what she does, from the excellence
of her existence, which is accessible to everybody.
What can really be 'mystical' there where everything
is so unproblematic and directly visible?" (KD, vol.
IV, 1, p.736)

With full agreement Barth cites the encyclical where
it quotes an ancient Church formula: the Church was
born on the cross from the side of the redeemer as a
new Eve and mother of all the living. What pleases
him less, however, is that "this 'new Eve' is afterward
with competent speed identified with the infallibly
teaching and reigning juridical Church, which would
have been compounded in the pope as the visible head
of this Body instead of in the invisible Christ". Again
Barth proposed to his readers: there is no such thing as
autonomous rule of the Church. Neither Paul nor
Peter led the Church as Christ's vicar. All they had to
do was to *serve* the Master.

The absolute primacy of God's revelation in Christ
also has its consequences for Barth's concept of the
sanctity of the Church. Every move toward independence in the Church must of necessity banish real
sanctity, he thinks. The Church after all cannot
become a communion of saints simply because a man
is baptized, thus receives the Holy Spirit, comes to
the true faith and as a member of the Body of Christ

would also become a holy member of this holy community. Against such a concept, Barth feels there must be a determined protest, because "The question of the Master's own activity in calling the community together is here almost criminally neglected." The really spiritual mystery of the holy community is thus being replaced by some wantonly invented sacramental mystery. What a strange concept does one manifest here about the Holy Ghost, His presence and His activity, about the raising up to faith, the belonging to the Body of Christ and therefore also about the sanctity of the member of the community, as of consequence of which all this would be communicated to man simply by the correctness of an action performed by men?" (KD, vol. IV, 1, p.777)

Clearly here also, Barth is still always extremely on his guard against any violation of God's sovereignty in Christ and therefore also against every form of absolutizing the creature. This is also expressed in the questions that he asks Catholic ecclesiology regarding its concept of the apostolic character of the Church. This cannot really be a question of automatic succession, he feels. A human being, even if he is a bishop, cannot simply by a ritual act "pass on" to his subordinate clergy the Holy Spirit whom the apostles received from the Master, and in whose power they proclaimed Him (KD, vol. IV, 1, p.800). All this is linked up with our concept of the Holy Spirit. As long as one sees the Holy Spirit as a kind of supernatural substance, which at one time in the history of mankind entered upon the scene and which now— like some newly discovered natural energy—got in the hands of certain expert people who could arbitrarily make use of Him, then there is no objection to the above considerations. But the Holy Spirit is not like that. He is and remains free and He breathes where He will. Barth further wonders how one can possibly get the idea that the work of the Holy Spirit would be a matter of bishops and clergy. A spirit that is bound to concecration rites can never be the *Holy* Spirit.

In a Foreword of 1955, Barth takes his Catholic readers aside for a moment. Explicitly he warns us then: "You will still notice a little of the distant rumble of the thunderstorm of the 1921 *Römerbrief,* even in the somewhat more friendly sounds in which I am now expressing myself on the things that you have very much at heart." The atmospheric disturbances to which he refers here and which continue to come floating our way from the direction of the *Römerbrief* have their effect especially in ecclesiology. Barth seems compelled by a kind of phobia especially not to give too much honor to a creature at the expense of the sovereign God. In spite of the happy introduction of the concept "sacrament", the work of salvation remains in the end always a continually renewed divine intervention from above. From this one can also understand that a Catholic author like Hamer reproached Barth for a kind of theological occasionalism. This characterization could even be repeated, now that Barth during the latter years has come back after all from the concept "sacrament" that we had hailed with so much joy. In the same Preface of 1955, he says that also his readers will undoubtedly have noticed in the second and third volumes that this general concept "with which in the first volume I have dallied somewhat self-assuredly and carelessly" is ever less frequently used in his studies and finally has been eliminated altogether. For the time being he leaves us in doubt about the reasons for this, although he does indicate it has something to do with the fact that "if anywhere then in this matter [he] has learned to hold such a thing as a guarded demythologizing as practicable".

Barth promised to come back to this explicitly in the treatment of baptism and last supper at the conclusion of the fourth volume. Following this announcement he wrote further: "I do have some suspicion as to what insinuations I am already now exposing myself. Apart from the angels, also the *Evangelisch-Lutherische Kirchenzeitung* has probably known for a long time that it would end up in this. But after all one has to suffer things like that quietly." Meanwhile the promised conclusion of the fourth volume has not yet been published. If the rumors are correct that Barth has given up the further completion of his *Dogmatik* since the incidents concerning his resignation and succession, then all this will unfortunately probably remain unclarified.

The thunderstorm that rose from Barth's commentary on the Epistle to the Romans (*Römerbrief*) has indeed subsided, but in its place there now blows a constant strong breeze. To put it more factually, Barth has never completely repudiated himself. Neither does he in the least appreciate it, if by all means one wants to assume any such remarkable developments in his way of thinking, or that he has now begun to call white what he once saw as black and vice versa. And rightly so. There certainly is an important maturation. How could it be otherwise in a theologian of his stature—also indeed of his times. The polemic attitude of the first period has unmistakably given way to a more synthetic, consistently christocentric approach to all the divisions of theology. His view in many spheres has become milder and more understanding. But it is altogether unrealistic to accept that he would have been making such a formidable turnabout, that one might speak with some justification of a total and radical reconciliation between Barth and Rome. Looking back on the last ten years of his activity he asked himself, with a certain amazement, at the occasion of the positive reception that has been given to his work among Catholics, "Has the millenium already begun or is it close at hand? How one would love to believe it!"

Notwithstanding many positive ideas that Barth has brought forward about the Church, for the time being he definitely does not want to hear of an agreement between his teaching and that of Catholic ecclesiology. This then—until such time as the contrary would be expresed—is a clear and definitive word. One may speculate on the question of whether with a better knowledge of modern Catholic ideas about the Church he would have given the same apodictic judgment. Apart from speculating about this, one can also pursue one's studies and make a further attempt to uncover the basic intention of both Barth and the Catholic teaching on the Church, and this will certainly have to be done in the future. Perhaps another Küng will someday be able to demonstrate that even on this precarious point the ideas of Barth and Rome do not have to be Church-splitting. This is a beautiful fantasy, but at the same time it is a very real possibility. It is therefore better to study than to indulge at such an obviously premature stage in shouts of joy, and in this connection the remark should also be made that even premature shouts of joy are always still a little more stimulating than the *Non possumus* chorus in A-minor one still hears from time to time from behind the denominational barricades.

A future study will have the task to enter more deeply into the christological suppositions from which both Barth's doctrine on the Church and the Catholic ecclesiology ultimately draw their inspiration. Barth himself has pointed this out and in the last volumes of his *Dogmatik* that have so far been published he has gone deeply into the doctrine of the redemptive incarnation. In conclusion of this broad review we still must dwell for a moment on this question. It will probably turn out that everything depends on how one judges the humanity of Christ. Barth as well as Catholic theology accept the definitions of the Council of Chalcedon as a matter of faith. With this, one accepts that it can and must be said of this concrete figure, Jesus Christ, that He is God. In Him time and eternity have been bridged, and although even in Christ the infinitely qualitative distinction between God (above) and man (below) has been maintained, there certainly cannot be here, at least, a question of separation. The centuries-long christological disputes of the early Church have made it clear to us, that an overemphasis of the separation between divinity and humanity in Christ leads to the error of Nestorianism, just as a too great stress on the union between the two leads to Monophysitism.

Following upon the fundamental intuition of his *Römerbrief* one would expect in Barth more of a tendency toward Nestorianism. It is obvious that—while avoiding *heteredox* exaggerations—he will still stress more that through which God and man, even in Christ, are distinguished, just as he expects from Catholic christology and, consequently, also from its ecclesiology that there will be a tendency toward Monophysitism. If, however, one realizes that on both sides one wants to avoid the evident errors, it becomes necessary to judge with the greatest caution. It then becomes especially fascinating to follow Barth in his explanations about the humanity of Christ. He tries by all means to avoid the underestimation that the Catholic theologian, perhaps, expects in Barth. We believe that he finally succeeds in this and so has laid a foundation for a more positive—if always cautious—appreciation of the human element in the Church.

In the measure in which the Catholic is less conscious of the Monophysitic dangers that threaten himself in his ideas about Christ—dangers that become acute as soon as Christ's humanity is being identified too unproblematically with God—he is also sooner to be suspicious when he hears Barth playing the theme with all stops out: God is the subject of the incarnation. The active subject in the incarnation is not the assumed human nature, Barth says, but the sovereign God Himself. Neither human nature nor divine nature can possibly be the active subject here, because a nature does not exist as such. Subject is the Second Person of the Holy Trinity, the Son of God "in and together with His divine being", he then further specifies (KD, vol. IV, 2, pp.70-71). Insofar as Barth is speaking here about the incarnation as a unique fact, everybody will instantly agree with him. But what is the consequence of this fact? Should not one also say now that in the Person of Jesus Christ, God has assumed a human nature that now also—in the activity of Christ—has *become* a coactive subject? Since the incarnation of God's Son is indeed a fact, can one still insist so much on the sole activity of God, that Christ's human nature becomes almost minimized? Barth gives a conclusive answer to this, from which, however, it also appears that a possible controversy in this matter will not be able to avoid philosophical-anthropological complications. Barth replies: "Can one say 'Jesus Christ' and therefore God *and* man, creator *and* creature, without making clear to oneself and to others that one is speaking here about Him who exists as this man exclusively by virtue of God's creative *action* and therefore in the historical current of a *history*? Can one contemplate what He has *become* in and through God's action— namely, God *and* man—and lose sight of the act of God in which He *became* that, and therefore also of His *becoming,* and dismiss it as a mere supposition? . . . It is all-important that one does full justice to the *living* Jesus Christ. . . . Can the *being* of Jesus Christ, presupposing that we are here speaking about the living Jesus Christ, be distinguished from what in His existence as the Son of God and the Son of Man happens as an act of God?" (KD, vol. IV, 2, p.121)

By these questions it becomes clear that it is all-important for Barth to see Christ being-man as a continuous act of God. The philosophical-anthropological implications of this view should be investigated further. To understand the "being-man" as a continuous "becoming-man" is no longer something new. If, however, the relative autonomy of man would

be jeopardized here, there would be cause to protest. However, this is not a necessary consequence.
In the latest volume of his *Dogmatik,* Barth himself
goes so far as to consider the concept "cooperating
subject" as acceptable. He does indeed prefer the biblical expression "service", but if it can be said of the
individual Christian, that "as an active cooperator in
the work of Christ, he indeed at one and the same
time receives, assumes and possesses a personal
responsibility in its realization" (KD, vol. IV, 3, 2,
p.690), then the same thing can also be said of the
Church. The repeated rejection of the Catholic
Church as "a continuation and extension of the incarnation" (KD, vol. IV, 3, 2, p.834) really implies
ultimately a rejection of the autonomous self-glorifica-
tion of the Church. But on this point there is agreement between Barth and Catholic ecclesiology—
especially in its development since Vatican II. God's
activity, His eternally new being that supports everything, His creative assumption of Jesus' humanity
in His divinity, all this does not happen in rivalry with
the creature. The property of the activity that belongs
only to God is precisely that His activity in no way
detracts from created activity. On the contrary: it is
exactly *His* activity alone that enables man to decide
freely. The highest imaginable creative activity of
God (and an activity that we recognize only through
revelation) is that by which He personally united a
human nature with Himself. The maximum degree
of union with God, however, is here at the same time
a guarantee for the maximum degree of human
autonomy. If this were not so, then the whole life of
Christ as obedience unto death would have been a
"make-believe".

If one now agrees with Barth that all created things must be appraised theologically through the Person of Christ, then it is at least not absurd to see the human element in the Church in the light of the uniquely blessed humanity of our Savior. The humanity of Christ has indeed been uniquely endowed with grace. No other created being is united "hypostatically", personally with God. That is why in Catholic ecclesiology we will always have to guard against identifying too uncritically the human element in the Church with the glorified humanity of Christ. On the other hand every grace that can be given to man is a participation in the unique grace of Christ. Therefore, it would be equally wrong to look upon the human element in the Church in a purely negative way. Man's endowment with grace is a reality, but it is at the same time a created reality as well. That this is in principle possible is taught to us by the created humanity of Christ, which *was* grace and *is* grace. Hence, to underestimate God's activity in the created order would do injustice to God's majesty. Just as in the humanity of Christ the redeeming love of God assumed a unique form, which as such is completely distinguished from every other human being, so also the grace of the glorified Lord manifests itself in a unique way in His visible Church. That this Church is called the "Mystical Body of Christ" means therefore that this created grace only exists thanks to the one grace that is in Christ Jesus. Thus the Church is more than merely a space within which God's redemptive activity reveals itself: she herself is that redemptive activity in a created form, and therefore in a form that shows itself under a veil.

Barth's strictly christocentric vision shows many

points of contact with a consistently incarnatory view such as expressed in modern Catholic theology. When both Protestant and Catholic theology will, in the future, render themselves a more strict account of this and, moreover, will take greater cognizance of the results obtained *extra muros,* then under the direction of God's Holy Spirit perhaps the moment will dawn one day, in which the great word can be spoken: we have found each other in Christ. The long time-consuming theological work that humanly speaking still has to be done before that day, the tedious pastoral work needed to make this growing vision also penetrate the broad layers of the faithful, can ultimately be done only in this hope. To hope—if need be, against all hope—is a sign of Christian realism. To resign oneself may sometimes seem more realistic, but it is not a Christian kind of realism.

Epilogue

In spite of the attitude of reserve that Barth has had for a long time with regard to America he still crossed the ocean in the spring of 1962 in order to accept an honorary doctorate at the University of Chicago, where his son Markus teaches Exegetics. To express his thanks he gave some five guest-lectures, which were later repeated at Princeton. From far and near, even from as far as California, buses brought interested people to the college halls. Apparently even in the United States, Barth counts more sympathizers after all than one might expect, perhaps on the basis of Reinhold Niebuhr's somewhat sour remarks. Taking his cue from the impression that the Statue of Liberty in New York Harbor had made on him. Barth gave his American listeners at Chicago a lecture on the essence of true liberty. For an American, Barth said, liberty must surely mean two things: in the

first place, liberty from an inferiority complex with
regard to the old Europe; but also, liberty from a
superiority complex with regard to the peoples of
Asia and Africa. Perhaps with this Barth had already
touched a sore point. But he took an even greater
risk by adding that especially for the inhabitants of
the United States the concept of liberty should also
include: freedom from fear with regard to Communism, to Russia and to the supposed inevitability of an
atomic war. Alluding to considerations that he had
already made public at an earlier stage, he remarked
that ultimately freedom is entirely a question, in general, of freedom from fear of all the forces and powers
of this world and the other world.

If anybody has manifested this freedom from fear
by his independence of judgment it has been Karl
Barth himself. All his theological activity and what
one might call his political activity bear witness to
an almost grim nonconformism. Many people have
repeatedly fallen from one surprise into another. Each
time a new volume of the *Kirchliche Dogmatik* was
published there were new surprises in store for his
readers. One critic once sighed, "At this moment
probably only the angels in heaven know where the
road of this *Kirchliche Dogmatik* will ultimately lead."
In answer to this, Barth declared that he found it a
comforting thought that at least the angels in heaven
apparently knew. On the other hand, this liberty and
independence of action showed itself in a harmless
way also during Barth's lectures. Those who would
be listening to Barth for the first time at the beginning
of the term would not infrequently panic on hearing
his pronouncedly Basel-Swiss accent. Especially the
many foreigners would at first be close to despair. After

fifteen minutes Barth would then interrupt himself, shift his glasses half a stage higher and comfort the new students with the assurance that they would get accustomed to his pronunciation. However, he would not make the slightest effort to express himself in a more generally intelligible way. After a few lectures one indeed became accustomed.

Supreme liberty of the spirit alone does not yet make a man a theologian of great stature. Such a man must unite broadmindedness with a loving fidelity to God's revelation in Christ. What that really means can only become clear to someone in living contact with a theologian of Barth's stature. One may well assume that his fellow Protestants can still learn a lot from his liberty in fidelity, but it would not be fitting for us to go further into this. As regards the Catholic theologian, he may in the company of Barth suddenly become keenly aware that his own realization of the faith does not rise above the level of applied dialectics. One does not have to agree, one even cannot agree with Barth in everything in order to experience at least *that*.

Although Barth does not avoid complicated problems, it always remains clear that everything is being meditated upon in the light of God's self-communication in Christ. In that light one can and must sometimes inquire after the real *essence* of things. But this inquiry after the *real* essence can only be answered with theological relevance through the other question: for what end? The continuing presence of this question gives theology a certain fervor. That this notion is not synonymous with pious triviality or with dullness can be empirically realized on nearly every page of Barth's writings.

Catholic theology seen as a whole still lacks this fervor to a painful degree; it is still too little a "sacred" science, because often it is still too essentialistic. To ask the question what the relation of man and creation is to God is in terms of logic and philosophy the question for an "accident". Would one not too quickly— unconsciously—conclude from this to the "accidentality" of this question? For theology the question of this relation is a question in which the very *essence* of theology itself is at stake. Meanwhile there is no reason for pessimism either. All over the world, the renewal of theology is in full swing. Zealous historians are finding that concepts that were anchored in theology are changeable and not binding; exegetes repeatedly force the dogmatists who were accustomed to quietude to energetic activity; patrologists are rehabilitating people who for the sake of an unsparing clarity had been registered as heretics. If in this boisterous activity one wants to keep alive the intuitive knowledge of what an authentic theologian really is, contact with a man of Barth's stature and manner can be of great significance. We have no wish to canonize him prematurely. Like every man he has his faults and there are also among the Catholic theologians of this movement personalities who keep their lamps burning. The denominational make of these lamps is, however, not the most important thing. More important is that the oil be found for these lamps, wherever it may be: if need be, with Elijah at Zarephath.

DEUS BOOKS
Popular Paulist Paperbacks

Specially designed to fill the widespread current need for popular treatments of religious and social topics underlying the contemporary scene. Each is timely, stimulating, solidly informative.

THE ADVENT OF SALVATION by Jean Danielou, S.J. Since we say it is possible for those outside the Church to be saved, why do we insist that everyone ought to be a Catholic? 95c

UNLESS SOME MAN SHOW ME by Rev. Alexander Jones. A book to meet the need for Catholic biblical literature, solid in substance yet attractive in form. A surprisingly cheerful book on Old Testament interpretation. 95c

WHAT IS THE CHURCH? by Donal Flanagan. For the interested layman and for the priest who wishes to brush up his theology and to obtain fairly easily a bird's eye view of the fruit of some of the recent trends in ecclesiology. 95c

COMMUNISM TODAY: BELIEF AND PRACTICE by Victor Ferkiss, Ph.D. Presents to the average reader, in non-technical language, a picture of Communism, without bias or distortion. 95c

ECUMENICAL COUNCILS OF THE CATHOLIC CHURCH by Hubert Jedin. A brief and proportioned account for the general reader of the most important previous Councils and the issues they decided. (Available in U. S. only.) 95c

THINK AND PRAY by Joseph McSorley, C.S.P. A series of object lessons for those who are learning the art of communing with God. The central doctrines of Catholicism are covered. For group and private meditation. 95c

HANDBOOK FOR NEW CATHOLICS by Aloysius J. Burggraff, C.S.P. Contains all the "little things" new Catholics need to know which cannot be covered in basic instructions. Ideal gift for converts. 95c

LOVE OR CONSTRAINT? by Marc Oraison, D.D., M.D. An excellent and important work on the psychological aspects of religious education. 95c

CATHOLICS AND ORTHODOX: CAN THEY UNITE? by Clement C. Englert, C.SS.R. A clear and critical examination of the issues that have separated East and West, by a foremost authority on the Eastern Rite. 75c

THE MEANING OF GRACE by Charles Journet. One of the greatest living Catholic theologians discusses the doctrine of Grace, one of the most serious causes of disagreement between Catholic and Protestant theologians. 95c

MENTAL AND SPIRITUAL HEALTH by Frederick von Gagern. A renowned psychiatrist makes clear that a happy life and progress in perfection depend upon recognition of certain basic psychological truths. 75c

THE PRIESTHOOD OF THE FAITHFUL by Emile-Joseph De Smedt, Bishop of Bruges, Belgium. A summary of the role of the laity in the Church, specially significant in view of the present Ecumenical Council. 95c

A RETREAT FOR LAY PEOPLE by Ronald Knox. Monsignor Knox, in his inimitable style, gives a down-to-earth and sometimes startling view of our problems in the only perspective that matters: in relation to the love of God. 95c

HOW TO ADOPT A CHILD by Don Molinelli. A Deus Book original. Tremendously helpful book to guide childless couples along the pitfall-strewn road to adoption. How adoption agencies work, and their requirements. 75c

HANDBOOK OF CHRISTIAN FEASTS AND CUSTOMS by Francis X. Weiser. Combines material from Father Weiser's "The Christmas Book," "The Easter Book," "The Holyday Book." Covers the liturgical year, inspires fruitful celebration in the church and at home. 95c

THE KEY CONCEPTS OF THE OLD TESTAMENT by Albert Gelin. Shows how divine revelation in the Old Testament prepared us for seeing the truth through God's eyes, as it has been possible for us to do since the birth of Christ. 75c

CHARM FOR YOUNG WOMEN by Anne Culkin. The author's well-known Course in Personality Development for high school and college girls, now in book form. $1.00

MEDITATIONS FOR EVERYMAN
Vol. I: ADVENT TO PENTECOST 95c

MEDITATIONS FOR EVERYMAN
Vol. II: PENTECOST TO ADVENT 95c

Both by Joseph McSorley, C.S.P. The author reminds the reader of the simple yet infinitely dynamic principles taught by Christ, and helps him to progress spiritually through this series of brief daily meditations.

A PRIMER OF PRAYER by Joseph McSorley, C.S.P. Progress in prayer, how to meditate, cultivate recollection, and deal with distractions. 75c

HOW THE CATHOLIC CHURCH IS GOVERNED by Heinrich Scharp. This well-known Rome newspaper correspondent disentangles the complexities of the day to day government of the Church. (Available in U. S. only.) 75c

MARRIAGE GUIDE FOR ENGAGED CATHOLICS by Rev. William F. McManus. Sound and utterly frank, this book is an ideal preparation for married life. For engaged and young marrieds. 75c

OVERPOPULATION: A CATHOLIC VIEW by Very Rev. Msgr. George A. Kelly. A calm examination of a highly controversial issue, presented within the framework of sociology and religion. 75c

PERSONAL PROBLEMS, ed. Kevin A. Lynch, C.S.P. A series of helpful articles on a variety of emotional and religious problems. 75c

POLITICS, GOVERNMENT, CATHOLICS by Jerome G. Kerwin, Ph.D. Dr. Kerwin's thesis is that American Catholics must enter fully the political and social life of the nation. 75c

WHAT TO NAME YOUR BABY by John and Ellen Springer. A positive approach to Baptism, for future parents. Contains Rite of Baptism, suggested names, etc. 75c

THOUGHTS FOR TROUBLED TIMES by Walter J. Sullivan, C.S.P. Brief, helpful meditations for busy Catholics, on many aspects of daily living. 75c

WHAT ABOUT YOUR DRINKING? by John C. Ford, S.J. The renowned moral theologian presents a reasoned, scientific and moral approach to this widespread problem. Excellent for high school and college youth as well as adults. 75c

DIFFICULTIES IN MARRIED LIFE by Frederick von Gagern. A psychiatrist's advice to achieve a happy married life . . . and to help create through such marriage a bulwark to protect the new generation. 75c

UNDERSTANDING MARRIAGE by Charles and Audrey Riker. Ideal for Cana Conferences, college marriage courses, family life courses, and parish discussion groups. Helps engaged and young married couples understand themselves and each other. 95c

EXPLAINING THE GOSPELS by Wilfrid J. Harrington, O.P. A fascinating, scholarly, yet utterly readable account of the four Gospels . . . their formation, background, agreements and differences, authorship, literary construction and theological ideas. 95c

THE CHURCH AND THE SUBURBS by Andrew M. Greeley. The Catholic Church in America has shifted to the suburbs along with the largest migration in history. An informed, balanced presentation of both problems and opportunities. 95c

WHAT IS A SAINT? by Jacques Douillet. Like "What Is Faith?" this paperback needs no introduction to the many thousands who cherish the original clothbound edition.   95c

WHAT IS FAITH? by Eugene Joly. A paperback reprint of a clothbound volume that has been very, very popular with readers.   95c

THE SPLENDOUR OF THE CHURCH by Henri de Lubac, S.J. A meditative attempt on the part of the author to work himself, and his readers, into the heart of the mystery of the Church. $1.25

SHAPING THE CHRISTIAN MESSAGE, ed. Gerard S. Sloyan. This book gives special attention to the problems of the "new catechetical movement" of the last fifty years. It incorporates the answers that a number of educators have given to the most fundamental question of our times: how are the young to be formed, and not merely instructed, in accordance with the living message of Jesus Christ?   95c

THE LIFE OF FAITH by Romano Guardini. One of the foremost European theologians of our times analyzes what faith means as an experience in ourselves and others. He examines the relationship of faith to action, love, hope and knowledge, and the Church's part in fostering and preserving the life of faith in each of its members.   75c

JOSEPH THE SILENT by Michel Gasnier, O.P. A historical reconstruction of Joseph's life and a study of his spirituality. In no sense is this a fictional or imaginative work; it follows closely the Gospel narrative and takes into account the teachings of the Church.   95c

FREEDOM OF CHOICE IN EDUCATION by Virgil C. Blum, S.J. A challenging study setting forth the reasons why the State and Federal Government, to be effectively engaged in education, ought to distribute benefits to those who attend private schools. For parents, educators, lawyers and members of the clergy. **95c**

123

MYSTICS OF OUR TIMES by Hilda Graef. This collection of biographies of ten mystics of the past one hundred years shows that a life of spirituality and mysticism can be lived by individuals engaged in the ordinary pursuits of business and living. Each combined contemplation with active lives. Each profoundly transformed the circle in which he or she lived and each is a source of inspiration to modern readers. An original approach to an ever-inspiring subject: the personal life of man with God.   95c

A SELECTION OF CONTEMPORARY RELIGIOUS POETRY, ed. Samuel Hazo. In his choice of poems for this selection, Samuel Hazo shows how mid-century poets—primarily in America—have faced the facts of life within their own age before they refused, accepted or transcended them. The English Departments of high schools and colleges will welcome this book.   95c

WITNESSES TO GOD by Leonard Johnston. The Bible has become so well worn in our civilization there is a need for something to help you see it fresh. This is what this book helps the reader to do. It is written with liveliness and wit, yet with a full weight of expert scholarship behind it.   95c

THE FASCINATING FEMALE by Dorothy Dohen. Every woman, married and single, will recognize the problems discussed by the author and be interested in her suggestions for a happy family life. This book has been written for the American Catholic woman primarily. In it Dorothy Dohen blends psychological, sociological and religious perspective with unusual success. Every woman will want to have a copy.   95c

LIFE AND LOVE: THE COMMANDMENTS FOR TEENAGERS by Daniel Lowery, C.SS.R. This book is meant especially for high school students. The emphasis is that the duties and responsibilities of Catholic living should not be looked upon as just so many "do's" and "don't's". The challenge of the faith is to see how much God has loved us, and to respond to God's love. A splendid text for high school classes in religion.   95c

CHRISTIAN FAMILY FINANCE by William J. Whalen. Drawing upon a wealth of experience, common sense, and detailed professional knowledge, the author discusses home-owning, furniture, credit and installment buying, insurance, food, clothing, recreation, health, taxes, investments, charity, social security and retirement. A book for husbands and wives and all engaged in family counseling. **95c**

COUNCIL SPEECHES OF VATICAN II, ed. Hans Küng, Yves Congar, O.P., Daniel O'Hanlon, S.J. "To praise this collection of 51 Council speeches would be like praising Shakespeare or the Bible. . . . It will undoubtedly become a Catholic classic." **Catholic World** (A Catholic Book Club Selection) **$1.25**

A BIBLIOGRAPHY FOR CHRISTIAN FORMATION IN THE FAMILY by Mother Marie Aimee Carey, O.S.U. This bibliography is intended for parents in order to aid them in fostering a genuinely Christian family life and in fulfilling their responsibilities toward the religious and moral training of their children. It also serves as an excellent guide for religious teachers, directors of Family Life groups in their role of counseling parents of children from pre-school years through elementary school. **95c**

LIVE IN HOPE by Walter J. Sullivan, C.S.P. Stimulating encounters with St. Paul, Cervantes, Sophocles and Newman: these one-page reflections offer adventure among the masterpieces. Essays on **Macbeth, Hamlet, Winter's Tale, Troilus and Cressida, As You Like It,** and **Richard II** afford enticing meditations for a Shakespearean year. All essays are calculated to engender hope.

RETREAT FOR BEGINNERS by Ronald Knox. A series of conferences that Msgr. Knox gave to boys in retreat at school. This book reveals the author's keen insight and wisdom as he speaks directly and forcefully to young men. As has been the case for every one of Msgr. Knox's published works, whether they are addressed to a particular or general audience, this book will appeal to the general reader just as much as it will appeal to young men. **95c**

LITURGY IN FOCUS by Gerard S. Sloyan. How the liturgy is something quite distinct from rubrics, how the Eucharist is at the center of the liturgy, how the sacraments are not just passing events in the life of every Christian, but are daily operative in their lives. No matter what point or problem of the liturgy Fr. Sloyan discusses, each chapter implements the idea that the liturgy is meant to mold and fashion the lives of every Christian, that it is not merely the commemoration of what once existed, but that it is living and real.   95c

A KEY TO THE PARABLES by Wilfrid J. Harrington, O.P. Here are all the parables of the New Testament places in their original setting—the ministry of Jesus. Father Harrington demonstrates conclusively how most of us are surely unaware that the parables, as they stand in the gospels, may not have quite the same meaning they had when first spoken by our Lord. In other words, if we cannot to some extent at least establish the original sense of a parable, it is obvious that we are going to miss something of its true meaning.   95c

ECUMENICAL THEOLOGY TODAY by Gregory Baum, O.S.A. The ecumenical movement is constantly expanding in the Christian world and it is the purpose of this book to explain and analyze the significant events and theological developments associated with this movement. This book consists of 30 articles, each is distinguished by its creative approach to theological questions. This book is divided into five parts: Problems of the Council, The Catholic Church, Ecumenical Developments, Ecumenical Dialogue, Christians and Jews.   95c

A MAN NAMED JOHN F. KENNEDY, ed. Charles J. Stewart and Bruce Kendall. Twenty-five sermons—selected from 850 from 50 states and Washington, D. C.—by the American clergy (Protestant, Catholic and Jew). An eloquent as well as an historical record of the representative words and reactions of the American clergy. (Requests of sermons went to nearly 2,000 clergymen.)
$1.25

126

A GUIDE TO PACEM IN TERRIS FOR STUDENTS
by Peter Riga. Weaving his book with a strong thread
of charity, Fr. Riga both instructs and admonishes, touching upon the plethora of problems that plague today's
world: unemployment, racism, colonialism, human
rights, economic rights, underdeveloped countries, etc.
This book does not have to be restricted to Catholic high
schools; its message is broader.   95c

THE LITURGY CONSTITUTION with study-club
questions and complete text of the Constitution and
Motu Proprio of Paul VI. A chapter-by-chapter analysis
of the Constitution on the Sacred Liturgy for the many
people who may find it difficult at times to perceive the
full import of the Constitution. Six authors of special
competence, who had been in touch with the liturgical
movement for years, divided the Constitution between
them, and each took the sections in which he was most
competent. Through their combined efforts they provide
in this book the liturgical and theological context which
the Constitution presupposes and in which its significance
is perceived more fully.   95c

FOUR CONTEMPORARY RELIGIOUS PLAYS, ed.
Robert J. Allen. "The Shadow of the Valley" by Jan
Hartman, an original 3-part mystery cycle in prose and
verse, dramatizing the crisis of faith in the modern
world; "Once There Was A Postman" by Robert Crean,
a 1-act father-son drama of superb sentiment; "The
Broken Pitcher" by Leo Brady, a 1-act drama of con-
flicting loyalties set in a Red Chinese prison which holds
three American Air Force men; "Without The Angels"
by Robert Crean, a wacky 1-act comedy, satirizing "pat"
religious art. Preface by Pulitzer Prize winning historian-
novelist, Paul Horgan. Eight pages of photos from the
TV productions of these plays on the CBS and NBC
Networks. All plays adapted for stage production. 95c

UNDERSTANDING PARENTHOOD by Charles and
Audrey Riker. An informal and practical handbook
about children and their development.   95c

SOCIAL ASPECTS OF THE CHRISTIAN FAITH CONTAINED IN MATER ET MAGISTRA AND PACEM IN TERRIS by Mother Maria Carl Haipt, O.S.U. Adopted for implementation of the religious syllabus of the New York Archdiocese. Provides background and material and a discussion of concepts basic to an understanding of the Church's social teaching. Aims to open the way to a more enlightened Christian action in our times.   75c

THE ENEMIES OF LOVE by Dom Aelred Watkin. In this meditative and instructive study of the subject of love the author shows that human love (if rightly understood) is divine love translated into the terms of human experience. He examines the assaults which selfishness makes upon that love and indicates where and how they may be overcome.   95c

JESUS: A DIALOGUE WITH THE SAVIOUR by a Monk of the Eastern Church. Sometimes our pretentious and complicated apostolates of today create the false impression that the man of today cannot hear Christ without all kinds of explanations, rearrangements and especially without endless preparation. In this work, however, the author is able to make every man hear Christ from the very first word. In his forty short meditations he recaptures the words and scenes of the Gospel and succeeds in helping us rediscover and appreciate more fully that very springing forth of the Word of God.   95c

THE CATHOLIC QUEST FOR CHRISTIAN UNITY by Gregory Baum, O.S.A. A balanced study of the contemporary movement for Christian unity in the Church and other Christian communities, this work studies the new attitude this movement has produced in the Catholic Church. It will open new vistas for the individual reader who desires to widen his work for Christian unity and will give him a new insight into the Church's ecumenical task.   95c

D OCT 28 1965